DEAD FAMOUS

William
SHAKESPEARE
AND HIS DRAMATIC ACTS

by Andrew Donkin

Illustrated by Clive Goddard

Hippo

Scholastic Children's Books,
Euston House, 24 Eversholt Street,
London NW1 1DB, UK
A division of Scholastic Ltd
London ~ New York ~ Toronto ~ Sydney ~ Auckland
Mexico City ~ New Delhi ~ Hong Kong

Published in the UK by Scholastic Ltd, 2004

10 digit ISBN 0 439 98269 3
13 digit ISBN 978 0439 98269 6

Typeset by M Rules
Printed in the UK by CPI Bookmarque, Croydon, CR0 4TD

14 16 18 20 19 17 15

CONTENTS

INTRODUCTION

William Shakespeare died nearly 400 years ago, and today he is more famous than *ever*. He wrote his plays in a world without aeroplanes, television or computers. But the characters he created, and the stories he told, have held people's attention for the last four centuries. His plays are performed all over the world and they've been turned into Hollywood films, cartoons, comics, musicals and operas.

Everybody knows a bit of Shakespeare...

But did you know…
- Shakespeare couldn't spell for toffee?
- That he went missing for seven years?
- That he used to help his work mates dress up as women?

- That he once stole an entire theatre?
- That some people don't think he wrote anything at all?

This book gives you the low-down on the most famous writer of all time – and probably the most mysterious. So before we go any further, we'd better get a couple of things straight. Unlike most other dead famous people from history even the experts don't know everything about William Shakespeare. In fact, despite people digging for years and years, many things remain a mystery about our Will. As you read this book, watch out for the Man of Mystery sections – the story of Shakespeare is full of puzzles *no one* knows the answers to, and these bits will let you know what's a fact and what's not.

But there are lots and lots of things about Will that we *do* know. You can turn to the action-packed pages of *The Shakespearean Sun* for sensational sixteenth-century news reports, and you can even take a peek at Will's secret diary (it's so secret that even Shakespeare knew nothing about it).

So dust off your ruffs, and take your seats for the show: the curtain is about to rise on the life of the greatest writer of all…

ENTER SHAKESPEARE STAGE LEFT...

William Shakespeare, the most famous and talked about writer in the entire world, was born on 23 April 1564. Probably. Well, perhaps, but it might have been a day or two either side of that.

?? MAN OF MYSTERY ??

WILL'S MUM

We know the date he was baptized, but NOT the date he was born. And by piecing together clues like these and with a little bit of guesswork, we can fill in a lot of the rest of Shakespeare's story as well.

Meet the Shakespeares... They're the modern Tudor family

Will's father was John Shakespeare. Before Will was born, John had served a seven-year apprenticeship to become a whittawer and glove-maker. A whittawer is someone who works with white leather and a glove-maker is, er ... someone who makes gloves. John also dealt in wool and grain and (sometimes) worked as a money-lender (something which was not particularly legal).

Being a craftsman gave him a pretty good status in society, but John had other ideas. He had cobbled together just enough money to buy a house and was soon working his way up Stratford's social ladder like there was no tomorrow. One of his best moves had been to marry posh bird Mary Arden.

Mary was the favourite daughter of a very respectable gentleman called Richard Arden. She was actually the youngest of eight daughters (just imagine the queue for the bathroom in that house!). The family liked to boast that they could trace their family tree all the way back to the time of William the Conqueror. Mary had inherited land and money from her father – which came in dead handy when attracting husbands.

John and Mary had two children before Will but both girls had died when very young. So you can bet that the Shakespeares were dead pleased with their new son (even though they wouldn't have known he was a genius yet!).

The first firm fact that we have about our infant genius is that Will was baptized on Wednesday 26 April 1564 in the Holy Trinity Church in Stratford-upon-Avon. Babies were usually around three days old when baptized, so Will most likely made his grand entrance into the world on 23 April – St George's Day.

Will was born in the town of Stratford-upon-Avon in Henley Street, in what's now called a half-timbered house.

THE BIRTHPLACE

The house included a hall with a big open hearth, a parlour with another fireplace, and an unheated room that served as the workshop where John made his gloves and stored wool before selling it. Upstairs were three more rooms that probably acted as the bedrooms.

Home sweet home

Stratford-upon-Avon was a quiet little market town in Warwickshire with a population of less than 2,000 people when Will was born. The town was surrounded by beautiful English countryside but lay close to the cities of Oxford and Coventry.

In Will's day, Stratford-upon-Avon looked something like this...

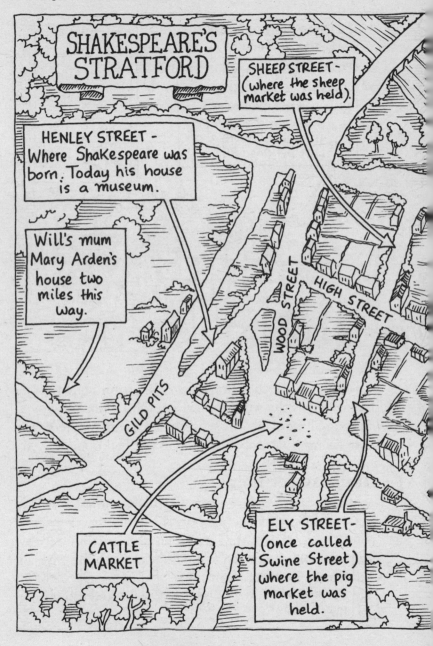

SHAKESPEARE'S STRATFORD

SHEEP STREET - (where the sheep market was held).

HENLEY STREET - Where Shakespeare was born. Today his house is a museum.

Will's mum Mary Arden's house two miles this way.

WOOD STREET

HIGH STREET

GILD PITS

CATTLE MARKET

ELY STREET - (once called Swine Street) where the pig market was held.

ROAD TO LONDON (fame & fortune).

NEW PLACE
Huge house that our Will buys later with money he's made in the theatre (we'll find out more about this on page 89).

KING'S NEW SCHOOL.
Where Shakespeare went as a boy.

RIVER AVON

CHURCH STREET

SCHOLAR'S LANE

HOLY TRINITY CHURCH -
Where little Will was baptized and (much later) buried. Now it contains a monument to him.

TO ANNE HATHAWAY'S COTTAGE-
Family home of Anne, later to become Will's wife (we'll find more about her on page 28).

11

Many of these old buildings still stand today and some of them, like the house where Will was born ('The Birthplace'), are open to visitors and attract millions of tourists each year.

Stratford had regular markets that sold animals and goods, and a number of shops including a tailor's, a shoemaker's, a carpenter's, a blacksmith's and places selling food. It was where a lot of roads met so there were always travellers passing through the town who needed to buy things like a nice new pair of gloves from Shakespeare's dad.

Until Will got famous with his writing lark, Stratford-upon-Avon was best known for:

- Malting – the roasting and grinding of grain ready for use in brewing ales and beers.
- Being very leafy. In 1582, some bright spark with far too much time on his hands decided to count the number of elm trees in the area and came up with the figure of over 1,000.
- Fairs – fairs could last up to 16 days when they got going. (They probably were a welcome break in a town that was so boring that counting elm trees was an enjoyable hobby.)

IS THAT ONE ELM TREE OVER THERE OR TWO?

Stinky Stratford

Lots of people died young in Will's day – only one in three survived to become an adult and 40 was considered a ripe old age. Here are some of the reasons why…

Although the town was small by our standards, 2,000 people living close together did create some very serious and smelly problems. For a start, they didn't have flushing toilets. That meant doing your doings in a bucket and then disposing of it – which often meant throwing it out of a window into the street.

With 2,000 people doing that every day (not to mention the market animals), things got very smelly, very fast. Because of this, 'muckhills' were set in several locations just outside the town. A 'muckhill' was a hill of … well, you can pretty much guess what.

People who didn't use them were fined, like for example a certain John Shakespeare (Will's dad) who was caught making his own muckpile near the family house instead of using the official one at the end of the street. John didn't care – he probably thought the street looked like a bit of a dump already.

Plague (or 'Aaaaaaaaggggggggh!')

Our Will was lucky to make it to his first birthday. When he was just a few months old Stratford was hit by the dreaded bubonic plague! The disease spread fast and ravaged the town, killing 300 people.

Here's what happened when some poor soul caught the plague:

Doctors weren't a lot of help either. The doctors of the time believed the human body was made up of four elements: blood, phlegm, black bile and yellow bile. Too much blood was often deemed to cause illness so a popular cure was to bleed a patient and let some out. This was done either by cutting open a vein or by the use of live blood-sucking leeches.

Other 'cures' included gently rubbing a patient's head with a dead chicken (how's that for a bedside manner?) while other quacks sold powdered unicorn's horn to make people better. As you've probably guessed, none of the 'cures' worked.

Unsurprisingly, the superstitious doctors didn't discover the real cause of the plague for a very long time. The killer was actually a bacteria that was transmitted by the bite of a rat flea. The disease-ridden fleas lived on the local population of black rats until they all died out and then (and only then) the fleas began to tuck into humans for breakfast. The bite of the flea was what actually passed on the infection.

This meant that usually there were not many rats left by the time the plague started killing people so they never got the blame. (Which was great for the rats, but not so great if you were trying to stop people dying.) Fleas could live in the bedcovers and old clothes of a victim for long after they were pushing up the daisies. This made the disposal of bodies VERY dangerous.

The plague was a terrible thing in Will's day. He never caught it, but the plague returned to, er ... plague him as a grown-up, as we'll find out later.

Top of the tree

Will's dad started to rake in the money. Gloves were always in demand (especially during a nice cold winter) and his sideline of selling wool was knitting him a small fortune too.

John also continued to climb Stratford's social ladder. First he was elected as one of the town's 14 aldermen. (An alderman was someone who helped run the town and made sure the laws were upheld.) Then, in October of 1568, John became the town's bailiff – its most important official (a bit like being a mayor today).

The roar of the greasepaint, the smell of the crowd

Around this time something very exciting happened – a group of professional actors visited Stratford-upon-Avon for the very first time!

The Queen's Men were a company of very successful travelling actors who had a licence to perform from Queen Elizabeth I herself. (Lizzy had become queen in 1558 and was the last of the Tudors to sit on the throne. Her father had been the multi-married fat bloke, Henry VIII. Lizzy never got hitched herself though. She claimed that she was already 'married to England' and became known as the Virgin Queen. She was also known for chopping people's heads off if they annoyed her.)

It's hard to imagine just how exciting this visit from the Queen's Men would have been for the small town. The locals had never seen professional actors before and just about everybody would have wanted a ticket. In one nearby town where the company had performed, the people were so desperate to catch a glimpse of the actors that a crowd had smashed the windows of the town hall just to have a peek at the performers.

And in coming to Stratford, the Queen's Men were making a tidy profit. Will's dad was the town's bailiff and was in charge of paying the company – they got nine shillings for their efforts. Thanks to his position, Will's dad was also guaranteed a front-row seat when they performed in the town's Guildhall. We don't know if he took young William with him, though.

If John did take William, this might well have been the first play that Will ever saw. So if you want someone to blame for all the plays Will wrote, maybe you should blame the Queen's Men because this one night might have given our Will the theatre bug for the rest of his life. (And given you Shakespeare for the rest of yours!)

SHAKESPEARE IN SCHOOL

As John was doing so well, he could afford to pack little Will off to school every morning. Going to school wasn't compulsory for children in Will's day. Sounds good, but that meant that many boys from poor families never went at all and so never learned to read or write. (Thus pretty much ensuring that they stayed poor.) Girls weren't allowed to go at all. They were taught at home but often didn't learn to read or write either.

IT'S JUST NOT FAIR!

elizabeth CAN'T Read

When Will was around five years old he would have gone to the local 'petty school' – a kind of starter school run by untrained teachers. Here boys would learn to read and write English and do a little simple maths. The main point of this was that the boys would then be able to take part in church services.

After petty school, your average seven-year-old might do one of the following:

1. GO TO WORK ON THE FAMILY FARM.

2. GO TO WORK IN THE FAMILY TRADE.

3. GO ON TO GRAMMAR SCHOOL.

Judging from the knowledge of Latin language and literature in Will's plays, it's almost certain that Will's dad made sure he took option three. There was a grammar school just a few minutes' walk from Will's home called King's New School.

Will would have used a quill pen made from a feather (usually goose or turkey) that would have needed sharpening almost every day. The class would have learnt using a hornbook made of wood and shaped like a table-tennis bat. On one side were the letters of the alphabet and the other was blank for writing practice.

A TYPICAL DAY AT SCHOOL.

6:30 – Start of lessons.

Latin – just the thing to help you wake up on a cold winter's morning. Pupils would begin their Latin studies by learning maxims (or sayings) by heart and later move on to read classic texts.

I hate Latin

8:30 – Break for breakfast – bread and a small amount of fruit. Then

Divinity – (Religious Studies) followed by

Arithmetic (in other words, Maths)

teacher

12:30 – Break for lunch – which might have been bread and a little salted meat. (Yum!) Then

Grammar – or 'How to Write English more Proper'.

Greek – a typical lesson might involve translating a part of the Bible.

Classical history – i.e. the Ancient Greeks and the Romans. (As you've probably gathered, schoolteachers were quite keen on the Greeks and the Romans.)

Rhetoric – the art of public speaking. Rhetoric was a favourite of . . . guess who? Yep, the Romans, who loved nothing better than a rip-roaring public debate. Being taught how to speak in public wouldn't have done our future actor Will any harm though.

ned

5:30 – Home time. HOORAY!
(And the end of a long, long day.)

Pupils got two weeks off at Christmas, two weeks off at Easter *but* (and here's the bad news) they didn't get any summer holiday at all! And schools were *tough* – the punishments were a little on the harsh side:

Crime	Punishment
Losing school cap	~ A good beating
Saying a rude word	~ A good beating
Bringing your sword to school	~ A good beating
Breaking any school rule	~ A good beating

Years later, in his play *As You Like It*, Will describes a schoolboy on his way to school:

...the whining schoolboy, with his satchel
And shining morning face, creeping like snail
Unwillingly to school

Was that maybe how Will himself felt?

Arms and the man

Meanwhile, Will's dad tried to continue edging his way up the social ladder by getting himself a nice coat of arms. The reason was simple: if your family had a coat of arms it meant that you'd really arrived. John applied to the College of Heralds, who were in charge of who could have coats of arms. (Only nice posh people, obviously.) John's claim for a coat of arms rested on a) having a good job (having been bailiff of Stratford), and b) having married Mary Arden, who came from a respected family. An application for a coat of arms cost money and John was starting to run out of cash.

For someone who'd spent so much time and energy trying to better his position in society, things were starting to go wrong...

The Secret Diary of
William Shakespeare
(aged 12)

June 1576

Poor old dad! What a mess he's in. He seems to be drowning in a sea of troubles. First, a few years ago, he was accused of lending money — something that's against the law. Some rotters claim that he lent John Musshem, a sheep farmer, £80 and £100 and then charged him £20 interest on each loan. (Sounds fair enough to me.)

As if that isn't enough, he's been accused of buying wool illegally! Only men called 'Merchants of the Staple' are allowed to buy and trade in wool. Maybe they might have turned a blind eye if it had only been a little bit, but dad bought four tons! (That's quite a few jumpers.)

All these troubles have been caused by James 'the grass' Langrake – a man who informs on other people for money. He is a slippery snake and no mistake. He was even sent to prison once for blackmailing the people he was informing on! What a rat!

Cursing him doesn't make things better for poor old dad though. I just wish I were old enough to help.

There may have been other reasons for supergrass James Langrake telling tales on John Shakespeare, though. Some people have suggested that John was being persecuted for having Catholic sympathies. Religion in Shakespeare's England was a bit of a hot potato. Here's why…

For the last 30 years or so, England had been chopping and changing between being Catholic and being Protestant. The trouble had started when Henry VIII had had a huge row with the Pope, the head of the Catholic

Church. He'd got fed up because the Pope wouldn't give him a divorce and so he'd decided to create a church of his own – the Church of England. Ever since then, supporters of both religions had been trying to get a monarch on the throne who was on their side.

Queen Lizzy had pretended to be Catholic for a quiet life when she was younger, but as soon as she became queen she changed both herself and England into Protestants! (She was sneaky like that.) A person's religion could cause them a lot of trouble.

John stopped attending council meetings and was eventually replaced as one of the town's aldermen – which may have been to do with his religion as well. In November 1578 John sold some land to raise money and shortly afterwards had to mortgage some of Mary's inheritance, as well as borrow £40 (equal to about £25,000 today!). John was getting more and more into debt.

The cast grows

John Shakespeare also had more mouths to feed than ever before. A family portrait of our Will's clan would have looked something like this...

DAD

GILBERT - AGED 13

WILLIAM - AGED 15 - OLDEST SURVIVING CHILD

MUM

EDMUND - SOON TO ARRIVE

JOAN - AGED 10 (NAMED AFTER HER LATE SISTER)

RICHARD - AGED 5

The Shakespeare Family 1579

Peasant or pupil?

It's sometimes said that Shakespeare didn't have much of an education. It's certainly true that our Will never went to university, but it's important to realize that he was far from being the uneducated genius that some history books like to pretend. He came from a good family, his dad was a successful businessman (well, mostly), his mother was the daughter of a nobleman, and most importantly he did get a good schooling.

Will was 15 when he left school. As money was in short supply at the time he was immediately drafted in to help with his dad's glove-making business. Just because he now had a job didn't mean Will would be without adventures, though. In fact, Will was about to spring a very big surprise on his entire family...

SHAKESPEARE IN LOVE

When William was 18 he did something that no one was expecting. He got married!

In the eyes of the law Will was still classed as a minor and he had to get permission from his dad to do it. He'd obviously been doing a few things without his dad's permission though, because his bride-to-be was already three months pregnant!

The lady's name was Anne Hathaway and the most surprising thing about her (apart from the bump) was that she was 26. At a time when not that many people lived to reach 40, 26 was considered quite old for a woman still to be single. We don't know what Will's parents thought but the age gap between the pair might not have best pleased them. So who was this woman who'd captured our hero's heart?

The Village Idiot's Ten-second Guide to...
Anne Hathaway

Hathaway Family Productions Proudly Present
ANNE HATHAWAY

Age: 26 (eight years older than Will)

Family: Anne was one of seven children (three daughters and four sons) and the daughter of Richard Hathaway, a farmer from Shottery, about a mile from Stratford.

Home: A 12-room house called 'Hewlands' that still exists and is open to visitors today. It's known as 'Anne Hathaway's Cottage' although in fact it's a pretty big farmhouse.

Distinguishing features: Er ... a bump.

The Secret Diary of William Shakespeare

November 1582

Blimey! Things have happened very quickly and I am about to be a husband! Yesterday afternoon I slipped away from dad's glove-making workshop a bit early to go and see Anne, who surprised me with some extraordinary news. I'm going to be a father! Of course I did the honourable thing and dropped to one knee to propose.

This morning I took mum and dad aside to tell them the happy news (and ask their permission to marry!). At first mother just kept repeating Anne's age while shaking her head, but father interrupted and said, 'First things, first. Does she come with any money?' When I was able to answer that she was from good stock and came with the sum of ten marks, dad shouted, 'Congratulations, my lad!' and slapped me on the back. (Mum gave him a bit of a hard stare afterwards.)

Anne's bump is getting bigger all the time so we need to marry quickly, but my youth has caused complications.

Two friends of the Hathaway family (who I think are glad to see Anne finally married) had to travel 20 miles to Worcester just to get a special licence because we're in such a rush to get hitched before the baby arrives.

I love Anne, but I am a little young to have the responsibilities of a wife and child so suddenly. I hope I'm doing the right thing?

??MAN OF MYSTERY??

WAS WILL DEEPLY IN LOVE WITH ANNE?

SIGH

...OR DID HE JUST GO THROUGH WITH THE MARRIAGE BECAUSE THERE WAS A SPROG ON THE WAY?

SIGH

On 27 November 1582 the Bishop of Worcester's register recorded the following entry:

> *William Shagspere and Anne Hathwey of Stratford in the Dioces of Worcester hath been given a license to marry after just one reading of the banns.*

'Banns' were read out in church to announce the upcoming marriage and to make sure that no one had any legal objections to it. This was usually done three times, but Will's unusual licence, granted because Anne was pregnant, meant it only had to be done once. So they could get married almost immediately.

Which is what they did.

WILL'S WORDS

You might have noticed the spelling of Will's name above. It wasn't a mistake by the clerk who filled in the register. (Although Lord knows he made enough of those.) In Will's day, the spelling of names was a lot more ... well, changeable than it is today. Six different signatures belonging to Will have survived to the modern day. All of them are spelt differently.

SHAKESPEARE'S ACTUAL WRITING

William Shackper

William Shakspear

Wm Shakspea

Willm Shakspere

William Shackspere

By me William Shakspeare

Other family spellings included: Shagsper, Shxpere, Shakeshaft and Shapeare. You can imagine that with everyone spelling their name however they fancied, things could sometimes get very confusing. No one knows which spelling William really preferred.

You might also have noticed that the greatest literary genius of all time had terrible handwriting! Yep, probably even worse than *yours*. It was shaky, scrawny, and looked rather like someone had dipped a dying spider in ink and left it to wander across the paper.

Shakespeare's first production

Six months after they were married, Anne gave birth to a daughter who they named Susanna. She was baptized on 26 May 1583.

We don't know too much about Susanna's life, but she seems to have had a normal upbringing in Stratford, living with her mum and her grandparents. We do know that she was in dead trouble for a bit when she was 23 as she appears in the town records on a list of people who didn't turn up for church services over Easter! (Shock! Horror!) She got herself off the hook though. A year later, in 1607, she got married to a doctor by the name of John Hall. He had a very successful practice in Stratford and the two of them lived to a ripe old age, producing one daughter, Elizabeth. It was inscribed on Susanna's tomb that she was 'witty' with 'something of Shakespeare' in her personality. High praise indeed.

The sequels

Two years after Susanna was born, Anne gave birth to twins who were baptized on 2 February 1585. The girl was named Judith and the boy was called Hamnet. (Yep, Hamnet – *not* Hamlet.)

In fact, the kids were named after Will's friends, Judith and Hamnet Sadler, who ran a local bakery. They must have been great chums because not only did Will make them godparents to the twins, but the Sadlers named their son William after our Will in return.

Judith pops up in the town's records when she got married to local tavern-keeper Thomas Quiney. The couple stayed together and over the years produced three sons (although sadly they all died before producing any heirs). Judith herself lived to be 77.

Sadly, Hamnet didn't do quite so well. Shakespeare's only son died in the summer of 1596, aged just 11.

Final bow
When Elizabeth (Susanna's daughter and Will's granddaughter) died at the age of 62 she was Will's last direct descendant. That means that sadly there are none of his great-great-great-great-great-great-etc-etc children around today.

Shakespeare's DNA might have disappeared from the world, but back in the sixteenth century something even stranger was about to happen. After the birth of the twins, William Shakespeare was about to perform a vanishing act and slip out of sight completely…

THE LOST YEARS

Remember at the beginning when we said that the experts don't know as much as they'd like to about our boy Will? Little details like what day he was born? Well, now we've got to the bit where they start to pull their hair out and set fire to their underwear. Here's why...

We know that in 1585 Will was living in Henley Street in Stratford-upon-Avon with his wife, daughter and young twins. We know that in 1592 he was working as a writer in London having his plays performed. What we don't know (and what NOBODY knows) is where he was and what he was doing for the seven years in between!

This period in Will's life is known as the 'Lost Years' or 'Missing Years'. There are few people quite so famous who have such a mysterious blank in their lives. William Shakespeare is one of the most important men who ever lived, so it's rather embarrassing for the la-de-da experts and history buffs to have absolutely no idea what he was up to for such a long time.

Many libraries, country houses, town halls, stately homes, and just about anywhere else you could think of, have been searched in the hunt for clues. But after several centuries of looking, no one has found any decisive evidence to show what Will was up to. (By the way, finding a sixteenth-century diary that spills the beans on Shakespeare's missing years would make you slightly more money than winning the lottery!)

Of course the fact that we don't know what Will was up to hasn't stopped people having a guess. (And some of them are pretty wild.)

?? MAN OF MYSTERY ??

HE WAS PROBABLY ON A SECRET SPYING MISSION!

OR MAYBE HE WAS KIDNAPPED BY PIRATES!

All of the following are possible but remember there's no evidence that any of them are what really happened...

1 Will the home boy

Perhaps the most straightforward theory is that Will did nothing. Or rather that he did nothing except carry on with his normal life. He might have spent those years becoming an apprentice glove-maker in his father's business and looking after his family in Stratford.

2 Shakespeare in law

Maybe he studied Law somewhere? Many of Will's plays contain references to legal bits and bobs and it has been suggested that he might have spent time working in the office of a country attorney.

3 'Please, Sir!'

Did Will become a teacher? One report from the son of an actor who had worked with Will said that he was 'in his younger years a schoolmaster in the country'. The only trouble is that the source who recorded it wasn't too reliable.

4 Shakespeare the soldier

Did Will join the army? A few people have suggested that he became a soldier in the English army. The English were having a series of scraps with the Spanish at the time and soldiers were much in demand. Once again though, there's not a jot of evidence.

5 To boldly go where no man hath gone before...
One rather romantic notion explains Will's vanishing act by sending him literally round the world. It suggests he might have sailed with Sir Francis Drake on the *Golden Hind*. It's a great idea, two such important and famous Englishmen voyaging across unknown oceans together, but unfortunately it's not likely to have happened – Will is never mentioned as having been on board any of Drake's ships.

6 Shakespeare the traveller
Italy features in nearly half of all Will's plays and its customs are described so well that some have suggested that Will may have spent at least some of his missing years travelling around the country.

OOO!

Invasion!

Whatever Will did or didn't get up to for his 'missing years', they were exciting and dangerous times for England and especially for the Queen.

For several years King Philip II of Spain had been planning a little surprise for Lizzy called 'The Enterprise of England'. But this surprise didn't involve balloons and a cake. It was a Catholic crusade to conquer England and replace Protestant Queen Lizzy with Catholic Mary Queen of Scots, who was currently banged up in prison. Eventually Lizzy got so fed up with Mary plotting against her that she lost her patience and Mary lost her head. This only led to bigger trouble though. Much bigger...

THE SHAKESPEAREAN SUN
July 1588
GOT'CHA! SPANISH SUNK!

Spanish plans to invade England were sunk today as the Spanish Armada was blasted, battered, and blown to bits!

The drama began when cheeky Catholic King Philip of Spain decided to invade England following the long overdue beheading of moaning Mary Queen of Scots. His armada of over 130 warships carried 20,000 sneaky Spanish soldiers towards our fair shores. The King must have reckoned that it was invincible, but he'd reckoned without the daring deeds of fantastic Sir Francis Drake!

Despite terrible weather, Drake sailed his English fleet out of harbour to meet the enemy. He didn't let us down! The Spanish ships were bigger than the vessels manned by our brave boys, but ours were quicker and easier to manoeuvre.

The Brits blasted the Spanish all week! Then came a daring midnight attack with fireships! Eight British ships were packed with gunpowder, set on fire, and sailed straight at the Spanish fleet! Spanish hopes of victory were going up in flames! Next day the two fleets engaged in a mammoth eight-hour battle and once more the Spanish got it in the neck!

Sir Francis Drake, known to his Spanish foes as 'El Draco', the fire-breathing dragon, had done it again. An impartial military expert said today, 'Bally marvellous! We really stuffed those Spanish swine.'

Let our readers rejoice at the news that altogether the Spanish lost 63 ships! (And we didn't lose any!)

Sun Comment: Better tell Catholic King Phil to cancel his invasion plans! Britannia rules the waves and Queen Lizzy isn't going anywhere! Well done, Sir Drake!

We don't know where Will was during the Spanish Armada but we do know where he popped up next. Will was about to move to the biggest, smelliest, most dangerous place in England. A city of beggars, robbers, and kings. A place of frightening squalor and breathtaking wonders. Shakespeare was heading to London...

SHAKESPEARE'S LONDON

London was like nowhere else in the world. It was the capital of England and its population was growing fast. When Shakespeare arrived, 200,000 people were living in the city. To put things in perspective, London had over 100 times the population of Will's Stratford-upon-Avon.

Conditions in London were sometimes incredibly cramped with most of those 200,000 people squeezed together inside the city's walls. (Several important things, like the theatres, were located outside the walls because there they did not fall under the control of the London authorities, the party-pooping Puritans – more on them in a bit.) The city itself was a maze of narrow twisting lanes that were muddy underfoot. It was dirty, it was smelly, and it was dangerous – with robbers and con men waiting to take advantage of the unwary at every turn.

Although many things about London were horrible, it had enough great sights to make it a popular tourist destination. People visited from all over Europe, sometimes for trade and business and sometimes for the excitement of being in a big city.

The Thames

The River Thames was vital to the city. In Will's time it was teeming with boats and ships of all descriptions. Tall three-mast trading ships would sail upriver and unload their cargoes from all over the world.

The Queen often took to the water in her dead posh royal barge and had herself rowed up and down the river just to show off a bit. A regular flotilla of up to 100 other boats would try and follow the royal barge up and down the river.

For normal people, wherries, or water taxis, were a good way to travel about in London, but you had to be careful. London Bridge had so many stone piers supporting it that when the tide was running quickly it created a torrential flow like a waterfall between the arches.

Apart from transport, the Thames was used as the city's source of drinking water. This wasn't the best idea in the world as the river *also* served as the city's sewer! (Ugh!) Most of the waste created by the 200,000 citizens ended up floating in, or mixing with, the water in the Thames. Needless to say, it wasn't a healthy combination.

Bright lights, big city

Londoners and visitors had a huge variety of entertainments to choose from. Most of them involved extreme violence of some kind. Here's a few of the most popular (and bloody) choices:

1 Football

Football was played with one ball, two teams and no rules. Large mobs would chase the ball up and down the street fighting each other. Favourite tactics included punching, biting and whacking people over the head with a plank of wood.

2 Bear-baiting

This charming form of entertainment involved crowds of cheering people watching animals tear each other to pieces. A bear was led into the arena on Bankside, and fastened to a pole by a chain before a group of five or six vicious mastiff dogs (bulldogs) were set loose and attacked the poor old bear. If the bear managed to kill one of the dogs then another was released into the ring to take its place. Some bears, like one called Henry Hunks, became celebrities if they survived long enough.

For a light-hearted end to the day's entertainment, a horse with an ape on its back was sometimes set running in the arena. The dogs were then released until both animals were caught and ripped apart.

3 Cockfighting
Large sums of cash were often bet on the outcome of cockfights – two birds fighting to the death in a mini-arena.

4 Laughing at loonies
One popular pastime over holiday periods was to visit Bedlam Hospital (real name Bethlehem Hospital). The inmates at Bedlam were all insane and people used to visit specially to laugh at them. (Kind, eh?)

5 Executions
Executions were a spectator sport like watching a stage show and they were very, very popular. The more famous the person, or the more horrible his crime, then the bigger the crowd would be.

The excited audience would watch the behaviour of the condemned man very carefully. He was expected not to shake or show fear. If the crowd were really lucky they might see the condemned man give away his earthly possessions, beg forgiveness, or (best of all) make some memorable final joke or quip.

There were three main methods of execution. Death by beheading was reserved for posh people. Things could get rather messy as sometimes several strokes were needed to cut off the head. (Posh punters gave the axe man a nice tip to make sure he did the job in one painless stroke.) The less posh faced being burnt to death (at least they were warm) and being hanged, drawn and quartered – the last method being an especially painful way of dealing with traitors.

Then there was…

6 London's theatres
People had also started going to something called the 'theatre' or 'playhouse'. (Perhaps because people enjoyed a bit of bloodshed off-stage, lots of the plays at London's theatres were packed with lashings of blood and gore!)

A quick history of theatre
The first theatres in Britain had been built by the Romans – but when the Roman Empire collapsed so did they. By the medieval times, entertainments were provided at fairgrounds, churches and market squares around Britain. These included mimes and miracle

(religious) plays. The yard outside an inn became a popular place to watch plays. (The audience could drink beer, and the actors could make sure everyone had paid to watch them.)

Throughout the 1500s, companies of actors travelled around the country putting on plays and, by 1567, the 'Red Lion Playhouse' was built near a farm in east London. It had a shabby temporary stage and fell apart after a year.

Then an important man in the growing theatre scene really made his mark...

James Burbage (1531–1597)

James Burbage was a carpenter by trade, but found it hard to make a living sawing wood, so he became an actor or 'common player' instead, eventually rising through the ranks to become the company's leader.

In 1572 a new law was passed which changed the life of every actor in the country, including James. Up until then, companies of travelling actors used to tour as they liked. The new 'Acte for the punishment of Vacabondes' insisted that travelling actors had to be under the patronage of a nobleman. (Patronage meant that a nobleman had to let the company perform using his name.)

The punishments for disobeying were severe (what a surprise). An actor could be 'whipped for many hours' and then be 'burned through the gristle of the right ear with a hot iron'.

James Burbage wrote to the Earl of Leicester (the Queen's cousin) on behalf of his company, asking Leicester for patronage. This was the deal: Burbage and his men would be protected by the Earl's name, in return, the Earl would have his name associated with the talent of the company and could show off to his posh pals.

James was a bit of a charmer as well as having a good head for business and just two years later, in 1574, he received an offer of patronage from someone even more important: Queen Elizabeth I! (Leicester would obviously have had to stand aside as soon as Lizzy expressed her interest.)

James Burbage grabbed the Queen's offer with both hands. He'd often thought about building a permanent theatre before, but a lack of money and those pesky Puritans had always put him off. Now that the Queen was his patron, it was the ideal opportunity to turn his dream into reality. The fact that he reckoned it would make, as he put it, a 'continual great profit' didn't matter at all of course. Racking his brains for a good name, James decides on 'The Theatre'.

The Theatre was the first purpose-built theatre since Roman times. It was constructed with wood and wrought iron, and could hold 2,000 people. It was built just outside the city walls so that the city authorities and the Puritans couldn't interfere – at least not too much. When it opened in 1576, it was an immediate success.

Cashing in on the idea, the 'Curtain' opened practically next door to 'The Theatre' in 1577. Ten years later, the theatre scene began to move south of the river as the 'Rose' opened on Bankside. And a couple of years after that our hero arrived in London. (In fact, Will had arrived in the world with a perfect sense of timing. Just think, if he'd been born just a couple of decades earlier he'd have got to London only to find that there were no such things as theatres!)

There's no business like showbusiness...

Plays were performed every day in London. When there was going to be a performance, a silk flag was flown from the theatre's roof to let people know. Just before the play started at 2 o'clock, a trumpet would sound to remind people and hurry them into their seats.

Prices were one penny to be a groundling (standing in the court) and tuppence for a seat in the gallery. There were even private boxes for hire for nobles called 'gentlemen's rooms' at the cost of a shilling. Money was collected as people came through the doors by a group of 'gatherers' – usually actors whose talents were not being used that day.

The Theatre had no roof and was open to the elements. Performances ran from April through the summer to October. Pretty soon thousands of Londoners were visiting The Theatre each week! The audiences that filled The Theatre were large and enthusiastic, much to the annoyance of...

The Puritans

The Puritans were a bunch of zealous religious nutters from the English Protestant Church who didn't like people enjoying themselves.

They especially disapproved of the theatre because they believed:

- It made people lazy because they bunked off work in the afternoon to go.
- It warped people's minds by showing strange things like boys dressed as women, and men pretending to be royal kings.
- It spread disease (especially the plague).
- It encouraged crime (especially robbery).
- It competed with church services.
- It was the work of the Dark Lord Beelzebub.

The Puritans were a thorn in the side of all actors and writers. Many of the city's officials were Puritans and our Will would spend the rest of his life trying to keep on the right side of them.

The audience

So who went to the theatre? Well, the answer was anybody and everybody. Lords and ladies went along with the poorest street beggars. It was one of the first places where rich and poor met on equal terms (OK, nearly equal: the rich had the better seats). Rich people mixing with the poor was yet another reason why the Puritans didn't like it.

The poor 'groundlings' standing in the yard in front of the stage were also called 'scarecrows' (because that's what some of them looked like) and ever nicer, 'stinkards' (you can guess why that was).

If you go to the theatre today you're expected to watch the play in silence; Elizabethan audiences were a *lot* louder. While the action was happening on stage, the audience would clap and cheer the hero and boo the villain. Whatever they were watching, audiences liked to get involved and make a noise! If they decided they didn't like the play or any of the actors then they'd start heckling right in the middle of the show. Sometimes they'd pelt an actor that they didn't like with rotten fruit or nut shells. Audiences were also keen on having a nosh while they watched a play. People known as hawkers moved around during the performance selling fruit, nuts, cakes, and bottles of beer and wine.

There was, however, a downside to enjoying a good play and that was the pickpockets. A theatre crowd was a great place for a cunning pickpocket to ply his (or her) trade. It was perfect because everyone's attention was on the stage and not on what was going on around them (or in their back pocket!).

Boys only

It was OK for women to watch a play as part of the audience, but ladies were not allowed to act on stage. Ever. No matter how good they were. Of course that meant that all of Shakespeare's great female parts, from Lady Macbeth to Romeo's Juliet, were played by *boys*.

Each theatre company included half a dozen boys aged 8 to 12 who played the female parts. That's one reason why plays of the time (including Will's) tended not to have too many female roles. The boys in the company were trained by the adult actors and spent hours learning female gestures and girlie speech patterns. Their careers were over as soon as their voices broke, so they could be very short-lived!

WILL GETS WRITING

No one knows exactly when or why Will started to write, but there are many stories about how he may have got his big break into showbusiness. Here are three of them:

?? MAN OF MYSTERY ??

A HORSE, A HORSE, WILL, FETCH ME A HORSE!

1 Four-footed friends

One story suggests that Will got a job outside the theatre looking after the horses of gentlemen. He was apparently so good at his job that soon people were asking for him by name. He didn't stay a horseman for long, though, because one of the actors struck up a conversation with him and was so impressed that he suggested the company give him a job *inside* the theatre.

2 Whose line is it anyway?

Another story has it that Will's first job in the theatre was being a 'prompter's attendant' whose job it was to tell the actors when they were needed on stage.

And perhaps the most dramatic tale...

3 Dead man's shoes

A touring theatre company arrived in Stratford-upon-Avon having just suffered a disaster! William Knell, an actor and one of their stars, had been stabbed and killed during their travels. Without him there could be no play! The company asked the townsfolk if there was anybody who might be able to take over the dead man's part at short notice. According to the story, Shakespeare was such a hit – with both the public and the actors – that when the company left town they took him with them!

As with so many other things in our Will's life, we'll never know the exact truth. However, it seems that by 1592 Will had left his wife behind in Stratford and was working as an actor in a company called the Lord Chamberlain's Men. He was also already writing plays. One thing that we do know is that it didn't take Will long to get noticed.

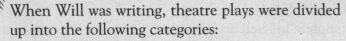

WILL'S WORDS

When Will was writing, theatre plays were divided up into the following categories:

Tragedy You can tell a tragedy by the fact that everybody dies in the end. Certainly at least the main characters (for example, Romeo and Juliet, or Othello) have to cop it. Shakespeare's audiences loved a bloodbath though, and more often than not (like in *Hamlet* and *Macbeth*) half the characters were dead by the end of the play.

Comedy Most comedies have a love story as their basis and a happy ending, with many jokes and often cases of mistaken identity along the way. A 'comedy' wasn't always meant to be funny-ha-ha like today, but they did always have a happy ending.

History These plays tell the stories of real historical figures, usually kings like Richard II or Henry V. Although based on fact, Shakespeare often played fast and loose with real history to make things more interesting.

Early works

Another thing historians don't know is how many plays Will might have already written by 1592. Some theories suggest that he might have made an early start on his writing career and got going during his lost years in which case he might have already written several more plays. Others think Will only got writing around 1590–91.

The first of Will's plays to be performed was (probably) a three-part historical drama with the catchy title of '*Henry VI, Parts 1, 2 and 3*'. Each play was complete in itself and together they told the story of the fifteenth-century Wars of the Roses – a long-running English war that had decided who would be king. The trilogy was a hit and made plenty of money at the box office – especially Part I.

Most critics think that the *Henry VI* trilogy gets better with each play, as the young writer learned his craft. The follow-up to the *Henry VI* trilogy turned out to be Shakespeare's first masterpiece. It was a play that would chill audiences for centuries to come with its portrayal of pure evil…

SHAKESPEARE SPOTLIGHT ON...
RICHARD III

Written: 1592

Setting: Fifteenth-century England.

What happens: Ruthless Richard, a man whose sense of right and wrong is as misshapen as his own hunchbacked body, is determined to become king. Several close relatives stand between Richard and the throne and he systematically sets about removing them. (Not one to hang about, he has already murdered Henry VI and his son before this play even starts!) First Richard has his own brother stabbed and drowned in a vat of wine. Next, he arranges the murders of the two innocent young sons of Edward IV. Boo! Hiss! Richard gets the crown at last, but disgruntled lords rise up in rebellion against him. He ends his life on a battlefield, powerless, desperate and utterly alone. Serves him right.

Best part: Richard III. He is a villain audiences love to hate. Richard knows his acts are evil. He tells the audience what he's going to do, talks about how skilful he is while he's doing it, and then afterwards reflects with relish on how well it went. It's particularly satisfying, having watched Richard slaughter his way to be king, to see him end up dying like a dog on the battlefield as he gets his well-deserved comeuppance. Part of the reason why people love this play so much is because the baddie gets what's coming to him. (And jolly hooray for that.)

Based on: Holinshed's *Chronicles* (a history book about England, Scotland and Ireland). Shakespeare's *Richard III* took real history and reshaped its events into brilliant drama. But Richard got rather a raw deal in Will's rewriting of history! In fact, Richard may not have murdered anyone, and probably wasn't a hunchback either.

Famous quotes:
'And therefore, since I cannot prove a lover ... I am determined to prove a villain.'   Richard III
Translation: If I can't be good at being good, I'll be great at being bad!

'A horse! A horse! My kingdom for a horse!'   Richard III
Translation: I wish I'd thought to order a minicab.

What a performance: Richard III is one of the great stage villains of all time and was a huge hit with audiences from its very first performance. In 1984, the actor Anthony Sher picked up on a reference in the play to Richard being a 'bottled spider' and used crutches and long hanging sleeves to give the impression of an evil human spider stalking the stage.

Will's rivals

During his early years as a writer, Will had some serious rivals. They were a group known as the 'University Wits' and they had several important advantages over our Will. The first was that they were already established playwrights before he even started writing. The second was that they were all smart alecs who had been to university. (Will hadn't, remember.)

Here's a quick guide to Will's writing rivals:

Robert Greene (1558–1592)

Greene was a jack of all trades and wrote stories and poems, as well as plays. His hobbies included drinking, swearing and chasing women he shouldn't. Greene didn't like the fact that our Will hadn't been to university and in 1592 described him as:

'...an upstart crow, beautified with our feathers, that with his tiger's heart wrapped in a player's hide, supposes he is as well able to bombast out a blank verse as the best of you.'

Translation: 'Ooohh, that Shakespeare! Who does he think he is?'

Green popped his clogs a short time after slagging off our Will. His enemies (and he had many) said that he died as a result of stuffing too much wine and too many pickled herrings down his greedy throat.

Today, his own works are largely forgotten and he's mostly remembered as being the first person to write about Shakespeare. A cruel fate that would probably have him spinning in his grave. (Cue sound of twirling corpse stage left.)

Christopher Marlowe (1564–1593)
Probably the most talented writer in London (apart from our Will). Marlowe's most popular plays were *Doctor Faustus*, in which a man sells his soul to the devil, and *The Jew of Malta*. Marlowe was also a government spy involved in secret activities. He attracted trouble like a plague victim attracted flies. Although quite brilliant, his luck ran out in 1593 when he got into an argument in a tavern about who was going to pay the bill. He was stabbed through the eye and killed.

Thomas Kyd (1558–1594)
Kyd was best known for *The Spanish Tragedy* – the smash hit play of its day. He created a new type of play, the 'revenge tragedy' in which a murder is violently avenged – usually with lots of blood. Our Will would have seen Kyd's plays and may even have used them as a model for some of his own. Kyd was arrested in 1593 after a search of his home found some heretical (anti-religious)

writings. He was sent to prison where he was horribly tortured. Kyd couldn't take it though, and ended up singing like a canary, telling his torturers that the naughty writings in question belonged to his former room-mate and best pal, Christopher Marlowe! Kyd was released from prison, but the torture was too much and he died not long afterwards.

Another playwright (but not actually a 'University Wit') was...

Ben Jonson (1573–1637)
Jonson was a bricklayer's son, and a lifelong rival AND friend of our Will. His best known plays are *The Alchemist*, *Volpone* and *The Devil is an Ass*. Jonson had a dangerous temper and once killed a fellow actor. (He was let off being hanged.)

Like Will he was a playwright, a poet *and* an actor. (We'll get round to Will's poems later on.) Jonson wrote slowly and was known to be jealous of how fast Will could knock out a play.

Whatsoever he penned, he never blotted out a line.

In 1597, Jonson wrote a play which was '*full of scandalous matter*' and was banged up in prison for a while. (He was let out later.) Ben Jonson became very famous in his own right and in 1598 our Will even acted in *Every Man in his Humour*, one of Jonson's plays. Jonson idolized Will and after Will's death wrote some very nice things about him.

When Will arrived in town, the University Wits must have seemed an impressive lot. Brilliant men at the peak of their writing powers. How would Will ever compete with them? Just a couple of years later though, Greene, Marlowe and Kyd had all played out death scenes in real life, leaving the spotlight free for our boy.

SHAKESPEARE AT WORK

But things weren't going to be quite that simple. In 1593 something happened that brought our Will's budding theatre career to a dead stop.

> ### The Secret Diary of William Shakespeare
>
> **May 1593**
>
> Disaster! The city has once again been hit by the plague. It's everywhere!
>
> When some poor soul is spotted with the symptoms of the plague, they are immediately confined to their own home. Their front door is boarded up and a large cross is drawn across their door in blood-red paint! It lets everyone else know to keep away!

I have heard shocking tales from Westminster telling how people dying of the plague lean out of windows of their homes to breathe in the faces of healthy people walking past. (Ugh!)

It seems to be worst in the poorest areas, particularly in the northeast of the city.

23rd June 1593
Curses! The authorities have ordered the closing of all the theatres in and around the city as well as the other entertainments like bear baiting. The plague spreads easily, they say, and large gatherings of people can only speed its journey. I can see their point, but no theatre?!

4th August 1593
It is a terrible time to be a writer (or an actor, come to that). The theatres have now been shut for months. Most actors have no way of making a living and are in a state of despair. The theatres will not be allowed to open again until the death rate falls below

50 a day. Who knows when that will be? (And soon it will be winter and the theatres will have to shut anyway.)

Meanwhile I am trying to make the best use of the time while the theatres are still shut and have started on a bit of poetry.

Shakespeare the poet

In Shakespeare's day, being the author of a popular poem was about as good as it got for a writer. Writing poetry was (at the time) considered a rather big notch above writing for the common knockabout stage. (Even if you do write most of the plays in verse, like Shakespeare.) After all, darling, poems were *art*.

'Venus and Adonis'

Shakespeare's first poem was a whopping 1,125 lines long and tells the tale of Venus, the Roman goddess of love and beauty. Venus gets the hots for Adonis, but the golden boy is only interested in riding around hunting things. The hunter becomes the hunted when Venus chases him, trying to seduce him with saucy suggestions like: *I'll be a park, and thou shalt be my deer: Feed where thou wilt, on mountain or in dale.* Venus doesn't even get a snog though, and things reach a tearful end when Adonis returns to his hunt only to be killed by a wild boar.

The poem was published in 1593, was an instant smash and was reprinted many times during the next ten years.

'The Rape of Lucrece'

Will's next effort was rather darker. Like many of his plays, Will nicked the plot of the poem from legend, but retold it in his own style. It tells the story of Tarquin, the son of a Roman King, and how a terrible wrong done to the lady Lucretia results in a horrible end for them both. Nasty Tarquin is banished and poor old Lucretia tops herself by stabbing herself in the heart. The poem was published in May 1594 and was another smash hit!

Will dedicated both these long poems to his patron, Henry Wriothesley, the Earl of Southampton. The following year Will followed them up with another long poem, 'The Phoenix and the Turtle', but that one never quite caught on like the others.

The sonnets

Over a period of about ten years, starting in 1593, Will also wrote quite a few sonnets (a particular kind of short poem). He must have been keen on them because he ended up writing 154! It was a format devised by the Italians in the thirteenth century, and really caught on as an Elizabethan fashion around 1590. Lots of posh nobles tried their hand at sonnets, but *no one* did it better than our Will.

Sonnets had a particular format. They were 14 lines long, and had a strict rhyming scheme. Here's Will's best known sonnet with its rhyming scheme.

1   Shall I compare thee to a summer's day?
2   Thou art more lovely and more temperate:
1   Rough winds do shake the darling buds of May,
2   And summer's lease hath all too short a date.
3   Sometime too hot the eye of heaven shines,
4   And often is his gold complexion dimm'd;
3   And every fair for fair sometime declines,
4   By chance or nature's changing course untrimm'd;

> Sonnets usually changed subject after line 8.

5   But thy eternal summer shall not fade
6   Nor lose possession of that fair thou owest;
5   Nor shall Death brag thou wander'st in his shade,
6   When in eternal lines to time thou growest:
7   So long as men can breathe or eyes can see
7   So long lives this, and this gives life to thee.

> The last two lines were often used to make a more general comment to the reader.

70

Line 1 rhymes with 1, 2 with 2 etc. This kind of sonnet is called the Shakespearean sonnet in honour of ... well you know who.

As you can see, writing a sonnet was a bit of a straitjacket. As well as following the rhyme scheme above, each line has to be exactly ten syllables long!

Shakespeare's sonnets are full of beautiful descriptions of nature, plants and animals. People who make greeting cards have been nicking bits out of them for centuries to sell to soppy-eyed lovers!

??MAN OF MYSTERY??

The first 126 sonnets are addressed to a young man, who the writer complains doesn't fancy him but fancies somebody else instead. The last 28 are addressed to a mysterious 'dark lady'.

Some people have suggested that these might have been real people and that the sonnets were the key with which Shakespeare unlocked his heart. They reckon that the love and the passion (oo-er) expressed in the sonnets were what our 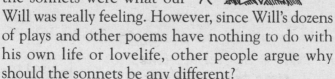 Will was really feeling. However, since Will's dozens of plays and other poems have nothing to do with his own life or lovelife, other people argue why should the sonnets be any different?

Whatever the truth, Shakespeare's sonnets stand as some of the best poetry ever written. They express an enormous range of human emotions about love, passion, jealousy and death.

🐟 WILL'S WORDS 🐟

In all his poems and his plays Will used an amazing 25,000 different words. That's quite a vocabulary, even for a genius. An average book might use 6,000 different words, and most authors would reuse most of those words in other works.

At the time Will was writing, thousands of brand-new words were being used in England for the first time. They were being nicked from Latin or Greek texts or were brought back from France or Italy by travellers.

Of the 25,000 different words in his plays, Will seems to have made about 2,000 up! (Or at least this is our first record of them anywhere. Without our Will writing them down they would probably have been forgotten for ever.) Here are just a few words and phrases that we wouldn't have had without Will...

Amazement	Eventful	Madcap
Assassination	Eyeball	Moonbeam
Bated breath	Eye-sore	Priceless
Birthplace	Fashionable	Shooting star
Cold-blooded	Fair play	Submerged
Countless	Hostile	Tongue-tied
Dwindle	Laughing-stock	Upstairs
Excitement	Love letter	

Some words Will used like 'ungenitured' or 'questrist' didn't catch on quite so well. Wonder why?

All change

London's theatres remained shut because of the horrid plague until 1594. It changed many things. Whole companies had fallen by the wayside during the long months of closure. What came out of the plague year was a brand-new set-up consisting of two main companies: The Lord Admiral's Men and The Lord Chamberlain's Men (the one our Will joined). It was the beginning of a great rivalry between the two companies.

The Lord Admiral's Men

The Lord Admiral's Men were based at the Rose Playhouse south of the River Thames. The Rose had been co-built by Philip Henslowe, who kept a diary. A lot of what is known about theatres in Shakespeare's day comes from his scribblings. (Along with recipes, card tricks and the odd magical spell!) Henslowe was a bit of a theatre whizz-kid, a bit like today's West End producers.

The Lord Admiral's star player was Edward Alleyn who, as well as being a bit of a stage legend also just happened to have married Henslowe's daughter.

EDWARD ALLEYN
1566–1626
Edward Alleyn had started acting when just a teenager and had risen to become the leader of a company known as Lord Strange's Men. He was an unusually tall man, about six feet (remember, people were generally a bit shorter then).

He was famous for his loud voice, which he used to great effect playing tragic heroes like Christopher Marlowe's Dr Faustus. People (mostly his rivals) used to take the mickey out of him saying that he shouted every line.

The Lord Chamberlain's Men

The Lord Chamberlain's Men began their life based at James Burbage's The Theatre. Will became their chief playwright and they staged most of his plays throughout the 1590s. Will wrote around two plays every year for them – while also appearing as an actor, usually in small parts.

When Shakespeare joined the Lord Chamberlain's Men he didn't just become a member of the company, he became a 'sharer'. Being a sharer usually meant lots of dosh because sharers got paid a share of the company's profits. Shakespeare paid £30 to become a sharer. Companies could pick and choose who could be a sharer. Usually they were star actors or people with money to invest. As well as the £30, Shakespeare had his successful plays to offer, so that's probably why he was invited to join.

Every month half of the profits were taken out and split between the nine sharers, while the other half went back into the theatre to buy costumes and props and whatever else was needed.

The Lord Chamberlain's Men consisted of:

THREE BOY APPRENTICES (to play the girlie parts)

SIX HIRED MEN (to do the backstage work)

EIGHT OTHER SHARERS (mostly the actors)

ONE MASTER PLAYWRIGHT - Mr W. Shakespeare

The Lord Chamberlain's Men included two BIG star turns, one funny and one serious:

WILLIAM KEMPE
died 1603

William Kempe was famous for playing clowns and fools. Any part that would get the audience laughing, particularly anything involving slapstick comedy, was given to him. He improvised some of his comedy parts (i.e. he made them up while on stage) and wrote some popular jigs that were performed after the end of a play.

Not everyone found him funny, though. It was said that he often annoyed Shakespeare by laughing at his own jokes too much. He was a co-founder of the company but left in 1599 when he had the sudden urge to morris dance all the way from

London to Norwich. The dance-driven odyssey took him nine days and was described in a pamphlet he wrote, modestly entitled 'Kempe's Nine Days Wonder'.

SOME PEOPLE WILL DO ANYTHING FOR PUBLICITY.

Audiences loved laughing at Kempe, but the really serious star was…

RICHARD BURBAGE
1567–1619

Richard Burbage was *the* leading actor of the day (and he was also the son of James Burbage). He became famous for playing tragic roles like Hamlet, King Lear, Othello and the murderous Macbeth. No one could touch him when it came to getting an audience weeping. He was said to have had a fairly realistic style of acting.

He was also (fellow actors watch out) well known for his quick temper. He wasn't just a clever-clogs at acting though, he was also a talented painter and produced many fine portraits. He must have been a close mate with our main man because he was remembered in Shakespeare's will.

Brave new world

After the long closure due to the plague, the way companies operated changed as well. Instead of touring around the country, some companies now had a permanent home. They were based in the centre of the largest theatre-going population in the entire world. Now the companies had the chance to build up a regular following of people who would want to see their favourite star actor playing part after part.

Staying in London meant that they needed to change how they worked. A company that's touring all the time only needs a few plays to perform because the company is always moving on to a fresh audience. However, if a company stayed in one place all year then they needed to keep punters coming back regularly to survive and that meant that they had to have more plays to perform.

Of course, that was very good news for one man; yep, you've guessed it, our Will.

SHAKESPEARE THE SUCCESS

Two plays a year – which was what Shakespeare managed – was some going for one writer! Usually one play was serious (which meant a tragedy or history) and one was a comedy.

HOW TO WRITE LIKE SHAKESPEARE IN FOUR EASY LESSONS:

1. GET TOP-QUALITY GOOSE FEATHER AND USE SMALL KNIFE TO CUT INTO A QUILL PEN. (YEP, THAT'S WHERE WE GET THE WORD 'PENKNIFE' FROM.)

OUCH!

2. MAKE NICE BLACK INK. USE ONLY THE FINEST GALLS (THE SWOLLEN BITS FOUND ON AN OAK TREE) MIXED WITH VINEGAR, GREEN VITRIOL, AND SAP FROM AN ACACIA TREE (OBVIOUSLY).

Easy, eh?

An actor's life for me?

It wasn't just Will who worked hard. So did the actors. The Theatre would have changed plays regularly – sometimes daily – meaning that most of the actors would have had hundreds of lines to learn every day.

Our Will would have handed over his original manuscripts to the theatre company when each one was finished. These originals were called 'foul papers' because the writer's own manuscript was usually foul with crossings out and corrections. (Sadly NONE of our Will's originals survive.) A scribe was then employed to copy out several 'fair copies' to give to the actors.

To save time the actors were usually only given their own part to learn, *not* the entire play. To help them out during a performance, a list of scenes (called a platt or plot) with all the characters' entrances and exits was displayed backstage.

When they weren't learning their parts, the actors were expected to help with the costumes, the props, and to set up the stage. When there was a performance they also sold the tickets, and sometimes the food and ales.

Over the years, Will would have got to know the actors very well and would have been in the enjoyable position of being able to write parts with specific actors in mind, making the most of their talents.

Mrs Shakespeare

When our Will came to the big city of London to seek his fame and fortune, you might be forgiven for thinking that he had forgotten something. That's right, *Mrs* Shakespeare. (Not to mention their three children.) There are no records of Anne ever visiting Will in London – although it's possible that she did. She seems to have stayed in Stratford and brought up their kids.

Although there is no definite proof, some people think that Shakespeare returned to Stratford at least once a year – if not more often. He may have written his wife Anne regular letters – although sadly none of Will's letters have ever been found. It's very likely that he sent money home, because as Shakespeare's income grew in London, so the family fortunes in Stratford improved as well.

One local legend in Oxford tells that Will used to break his journey between London and Stratford at a wine-house called the Taverne. A version of the story suggests that our Will had a fling with the landlord's beautiful wife and that they produced a son together. If it's true or not we'll never know.

Whatever the state of Will's love life in the real world, on stage he could turn his hand to romance whenever he fancied. In 1595, our Will wrote the greatest love story of all time...

SHAKESPEARE SPOTLIGHT ON...
ROMEO & JULIET

Written: 1595

Setting: Verona, Italy.

What happens: Two families, the Montagues and the Capulets, hate each other. Montague boy falls in love with Capulet girl. It all goes horribly wrong. Everyone dies unpleasantly. Simple really. Agony aunts often say that many relationships fail because the couple don't talk to each other. This was certainly true for these two:

1. JULIET NEEDS TO AVOID BEING MARRIED OFF TO SOMEONE ELSE AND COMES UP WITH A PLAN TO FAKE HER OWN DEATH.

2. JULIET GETS A MATE TO WRITE A LETTER TO ROMEO FILLING HIM IN ON HER PLAN AND THEN TAKES A SLEEPING POTION THAT GIVES THE APPEARANCE OF DEATH.

3. ROMEO HEARS THAT JULIET IS DEAD <u>BUT</u> DOESN'T GET THE LETTER.

4. ROMEO RUSHES TO JULIET'S TOMB. SEEING HER DEAD BODY IS TOO MUCH FOR OUR HEART-THROB. HE GULPS DOWN SOME POISON AND DROPS DEAD.

5. JULIET WAKES UP, SEES ROMEO LAYING DEAD AND... (YEP, YOU'VE GUESSED IT) SHE COMMITS SUICIDE FOR REAL BY STABBING HERSELF.

Best parts: Romeo begins the play as a teenager with too much time on his hands, but soon falls head over heels for Juliet. Juliet starts as a bit of a spoilt 13-year-old brat, but falling for Romeo makes her grow up pretty quickly.

Based on: Two years before Will was born, the famous poem 'The Tragical History of Romeus and Juliet' proved to be rather popular with the punters. So popular in fact that Will nicked the story for his play.

Famous quotes:

'O Romeo, Romeo! Wherefore art thou Romeo?' Juliet
Translation: Why did it have to be you?

'But, soft! What light through yonder window breaks? It is the east, and Juliet is the sun.' Romeo (obviously)
Translation: You're gorgeous, you are.

What a performance: There have been literally hundreds of retellings of the Romeo and Juliet story. In 1961, it was reborn as a sassy, American, musical retitled *West Side Story*. Film director, Franco Zeffirelli, created a classic film version in 1968 which won two Oscars. And in 1997, Hollywood refilmed the tragic tale with Leonardo DiCaprio and Claire Danes as the leads in an MTV-style rock-fest that had enough fast camera cuts to make you dizzy.

83

Her Majesty requests…

Throughout the 1590s, Shakespeare and the Lord Chamberlain's Men gave regular performances for the Queen. She didn't go to the theatre though: the theatre came to her. The actors would travel to whichever of the royal palaces Her Majesty was staying in at the time. And there were quite a few to choose from, including Greenwich, Richmond, Hampton Court and Nonsuch.

The actors would build a temporary stage inside the palace itself, usually in a large hall somewhere. The Queen (now in her sixties) could then enjoy a decent royal feast AND a private performance of a play.

ONE HOPES THERE'LL BE PLENTY OF KILLINGS IN IT!

Many of Shakespeare's plays were performed before Queen Elizabeth, and at least one was supposed to have been written specially for her. Apart from one occasion when he nearly got his head cut off (which we'll get to later), Will must have enjoyed performing and writing for royalty. Playing before the Queen was the highest honour that an actor or a playwright could receive.

ஃ WILL'S WORDS ஃ

As well as giving us a huge number of new words, Will has also contributed dozens of expressions which have gone on to become household words, like the phrase … er … 'household words'! Here are just a few phrases that people say without even realizing that they're quoting from Shakespeare:

'The world's your oyster'
started life as 'Why then, the world's mine oyster,' in
The Merry Wives of Windsor.

'He's eaten us out of house and home'
Was originally a line from *Henry IV, Part 2.*

'It's all Greek to me'
started life in *Julius Caesar.*

'Into thin air'
comes from the end of *The Tempest.*

'Neither a borrower nor a lender be'
Sound financial advice from the play *Hamlet.*

'To thine own self be true'
More advice from *Hamlet.*

'Neither rhyme nor reason'
started out as a line in *As You Like It.*

'The course of true love never did run smooth'
An observation from *A Midsummer Night's Dream.*

'Wild goose-chase'
comes from *Romeo and Juliet.*

'All that glitters is not gold'
from *The Merchant of Venice.*

A country boy at heart

Although now writing in London, Will never forgot the animals, birds, plants and trees of the countryside that surrounded the little town where he had been born. When he was growing up, Stratford was surrounded by farmer's fields, wild meadows and the great green Forest of Arden. Will would also have seen the yearly cycle of sowing and harvesting of crops at close hand.

Will's plays contain over 3,000 references to nearly 200 different wild flowers, trees, birds and animals. Many plants and animals were symbols of certain things. Often Shakespeare would use these meanings to add colour to his work. Here are just a few of Shakespeare's animals (all of them pop up in his plays) and what they symbolized for the people of his time.

A Midsummer Night's Dream

In 1596, Will drew upon his memories of the countryside to produce one of his most popular comedies, *A Midsummer Night's Dream*. The play is all about love. Two couples wander into a magical forest on midsummer night and find themselves falling in love with the wrong partners thanks to a fairy spell. Much silliness and comic confusion follow, of course.

Titania, the queen of the fairies, is also enchanted and falls in love with Bottom, a man who has had his head magically replaced with the head of an ass. (Yep, really.) Bottom is one of the funniest roles in the play and today the part is often taken by comedians trying their hand at 'serious' theatre.

Will used figures from folklore as his inspiration for the mischief-making character Puck. Puck is a shape-shifting sprite who represents the spirit of chaos and revels in the confusion that he causes. He has fairy superpowers and can cast spells, change the weather and circle the entire earth in just a moment.

Some people think that the play (all about love and marriage) was written to be performed at an important posh-knob wedding. Whoever he wrote it for originally, it has proved to be one of Will's best-loved works.

Act fact

In *A Midsummer Night's Dream*, there's a bit where some very amateur actors give a VERY amateur performance of a play with the silly title of '*The most Lamentable Comedy and most Cruel Death of Pyramus and Thisby*'. In fact our Will was taking the mickey out of a real play of the time written by Thomas Preston who had called his own play…

> **A Lamentable Tragedy, Mixed Full of Pleasant Mirth, Containing Cambyses, King of Persia, from the beginning of his kingdom unto his death, his one good deed of execution, after that many wicked deeds and tyrannous murders committed by and through him, and last of all his odious death by God's justice appointed.**

Try getting that onto a theatre poster!

A man of wealth and taste

In the space of a few years between 1590 and 1596, our Will had risen from being a complete unknown to become the most successful playwright in London. Thanks to his deal as a sharer in the company he reaped the rewards as well. Like his dad, Will was good with money and had been careful with his theatre profits. And he hadn't forgotten his parents either.

Remember how Will's dad had wanted to get a coat of arms for the family but he'd had to give up because of his money troubles? Well, Will was now able to do his dad a big favour.

Will had the money to get the family fortunes back on track and get the coat of arms that his father had always wanted. The motto on the coat of arms was 'Non Sanz Droict', which was a Frenchified way of saying 'not without right'. It meant that John Shakespeare (and his son Will) were now officially 'gentlemen'. Will's dad must have been extremely proud of him!

While Will was splashing his money around a bit, in 1597 he also bought himself a huge house in Stratford-upon-Avon called New Place. It was the second biggest house in the whole town and one of the most expensive.

It looked something like this:

It had three floors, five gables (pointy bits), loads of rooms, ten fireplaces, and came with grounds that included barns, gardens and fruit orchards.

Sadly, the house doesn't exist today. About 150 years after Will died, the owner got so fed up with people knocking on his door asking for souvenirs of Shakespeare that he had the whole building torn down!

?? MAN OF MYSTERY ??

We don't know how much time Shakespeare actually spent at New Place. For years it was assumed that he lived in London and only very occasionally made the journey home for a short visit with his wife and children. But some people have suggested that he might have started staying in Stratford for longer periods now that he had this fine house.

Although Will was a theatre animal and enjoyed company, writing takes peace and quiet. Perhaps this would have been easier to find in his new home than in the crowded, plague-ridden capital? Perhaps now he owned this building, Will spent more time writing at home and helping Mrs Shakespeare bring up the kids? We'll never know.

The long arm of the law

Will's plays contain many references to the law and to lawyers. So many, in fact, that as we've seen, some people have suggested that Will might have worked in a law office during his 'Missing Years'.

That's probably not likely, but it's certainly true that Will often had the law on his mind. Perhaps his father's own problems with the law had made a big impression on Will as a kid. After all, in his play Henry VI Part II, a rebel does cry: 'The first thing we do, let's kill all the lawyers.' (Nice idea.)

In Will's time, people started legal actions against one another just as much as they do today. People who worked in the law courts in London were also a sizeable part of our Will's audience. Little wonder then that for Will's next hit he decided to put the law and the legal system centre stage...

SHAKESPEARE SPOTLIGHT ON...
THE MERCHANT OF VENICE

Written: 1597

Setting: Fifteenth-century Italy.

What happens: Antonio (the merchant of the title) borrows 3,000 ducats from Shylock the moneylender. (You can tell it's a mistake already, can't you?) Antonio says he'll pay him back when his ships return full of goods. Shylock demands that if Antonio fails to pay him back then Shylock can have a pound of Antonio's flesh. (Imagine him as a bank manager.)

Of course, it's not long before the news comes that all Antonio's ships have sunk. (Doh!) The case goes to court and Shylock demands his pound of flesh. Antonio is defended in court by Portia (the female lead). Here you've got a boy disguised as a woman, but in this case playing a woman disguised as a man. (Read it slowly.)

Portia appeals to Shylock's better nature only to find he doesn't have one. When that fails, she falls back on the letter of the law. Shylock may have his pound of flesh, BUT only if he can get it without taking a single drop of blood. It's an impossible task and Shylock is defeated.

WOULD YOU SETTLE FOR A POUND OF TURNIPS?

92

Best part: Shylock. He's a Jewish moneylender and the play is obviously and deliberately anti-Semitic (i.e. against Jews). Shakespeare was reflecting the general ill feeling in Elizabethan England at the time, particularly against moneylenders. (Although remember that was what Will's dad had been caught doing.)

Famous quotes:
'The quality of mercy is not strained.
It droppeth as the gentle rain from heaven.'   Portia
Translation: Go easy, Shylock!

'If you prick us, do we not bleed?
If you tickle us, do we not laugh?
If you poison us, do we not die?
And if you wrong us, shall we not revenge?'   Shylock
Translation: Everyone's the same underneath.

What a performance: It's worth saying that just before *The Merchant of Venice* was first performed, the Queen's doctor, who was a Jewish immigrant, had been caught plotting to poison Her Majesty! He was executed. The resulting public ill feeling towards Jewish people might have influenced Shakespeare. Maybe he made Shylock the villain to do a bit of grovelling to Her Majesty?

In early productions (early means the first 300 years' worth!) Shylock was always played as the villain. More recent productions, especially since the Second World War, have tended to show Shylock as the victim of racism. One reason that Will's plays have lasted for such a long time is that is possible for actors and directors to interpret them in many different ways.

Will's wrong bits

Shakespeare was a genius, but he didn't get everything right. See if you can spot what's wrong with the following scenes written over his long career. (Answers opposite.)

1 *Antony and Cleopatra* – In one scene Cleopatra, the Queen of Egypt, suggests they play a game of billiards.

2 *Julius Caesar* – This play told the story of the assassination of Emperor Julius Caesar. In one scene a clock chimes dramatically.

3 *The Winter's Tale* – This play features a scene where a character goes to the wild seashore of Bohemia and gets chased and eaten by a bear.

4 *King Lear* – In this tragedy set in ancient Britain the Duke of Gloucester gets a letter from his son and he says that he must have his glasses to read it.

Answers:

1 She might be queen but that doesn't change the fact that billiards weren't invented for another 1,000 years!

2 Yep, you got it, they didn't have clocks back in ancient Rome either. Guess a chiming sundial was out of the question then?

3 No, it's not the bear, it's the seashore. Bohemia (roughly where the Czech Republic is today) was completely surrounded by land.

4 The Duke might have a castle, armies and the best horses in the kingdom, but the play's set in ancient Britain. Would he have had glasses? There weren't too many opticians (or pairs of glasses) around in those days!

Another new home

On 13 April 1597 the Lord Chamberlain's Men's lease on the theatre where they performed ran out. This meant big, big, trouble. James Burbage had to renegotiate the rent with Giles Allen, the landlord. They agreed the new rent (up from £14 to £24 per year) but when Allen demanded he have the building back after only five years, Burbage refused.

A desperate Burbage started looking elsewhere and found a site in Blackfriars in the middle of London. At the last minute, however, his plan fell apart. It was a bit of a posh area and the locals didn't like the idea of a common theatre on their doorsteps.

He must have been pretty disappointed because the next thing James Burbage did was drop dead. That left his son to take over the negotiations but the whole deal soon fell apart. Then whispers reached the ears of the company that their none-too-helpful landlord was planning to 'pull down the theatre and convert the wood and timber to some better use'.

Clearly something had to be done. And quickly. The plan that they decided upon was as daring as it was brilliant. The theatre company decided to steal their own theatre! Here's how they did it:

HOW TO STEAL A THEATRE

1. MAKE SURE YOUR LANDLORD IS OUT OF TOWN.

I'M OFF.

2. CHECK EXPIRED LEASE FOR SPECIAL SMALL PRINT SAYING YOU CAN DISMANTLE THEATRE IF YOU WANT TO.

CONTRACT

3. ARRANGE SECRET MEETING AFTER DARK.

Richard Burbage   Cuthbert Burbage   Widow Burbage (along for the fun)

Peter Street (chief carpenter)

4. DISMANTLE SAID THEATRE PIECE BY PIECE.
REMEMBER WHERE THAT BIT GOES.

5. HIRE FERRYBOAT TO TAKE TIMBERS ACROSS THE RIVER.

6. CHOOSE NICE NEW PIECE OF LAND.
HOW ABOUT OVER THERE?
JUST UP THE ROAD FROM THE TATTY OLD ROSE THEATRE!

The landlord was not a happy bunny. On the other hand, our Will and his chums were all smiles. They had saved their theatre and probably their careers as well. Now all they had to do was decide on the 'new' theatre's name…

SHAKESPEARE'S GLOBE

Everyone agreed on the 'Globe' – this was after all the age of discovery with sailors reaching uncharted shores all over the, er … globe. The Globe's advertising logo was very classy, just as you'd expect, and showed the Greek god Hercules carrying the world on his shoulders.

Will was going to have a new theatre where his plays could be performed and it got even better. The Burbage brothers offered some of the leading talents in the company the chance to own shares in the new building (not just the company but the building itself). Usually theatres were owned by the behind-the-scenes money-men so this was a first. Our Will, always on the lookout for a good deal, became part of the Burbage syndicate. (A syndicate is a group of people who get together to buy something.)

It wasn't long before word spread about London's 'newest' theatre...

THE SHAKESPEAREAN SUN
1599

CURTAIN OPENS ON NEW THEATRE

Londoners flooded south of the river today to see the city's newest theatre open its doors for the first time! The sumptuous construction, built by the Lord Chamberlain's Men theatre company, is called the Globe and can hold an audience of up to 3,000!

The Burbage brothers and London's favourite playwright, Mr William Shakespeare, have set up their new theatre in Bankside. As Londoners will know, the area is already an entertainment hotspot, with its bear pits, and cockfights. It's also home to the old and flea-bitten Rose Theatre, where the Lord Chamberlain's Men's deadly acting enemies, the Admiral's Men, are based.

The company were said to have been flooded with messages of goodwill on their opening night. 'The devil will take their

souls straight to hell!' said one Puritan leader quite reasonably.

The Admiral's Men were also generous in welcoming their fellow entertainers south of the river with open arms: 'I hope the place burns down with that lot in it,' said one.

Rivals

The Admiral's Men were very unhappy about Will's company coming over the water and muscling in on their

patch. The new Globe had been built only 50 metres away from the Rose Theatre! The Globe was a lovely new building, while the Rose was old and damp.

The Admiral's Men stuck it out for a while and then made the sensible choice of moving north of the river to build a theatre called the Fortune. It was a good idea. They entertained punters there for the next 20 years.

The Globe

The new theatre had 20 short sides stretching round to form an 'O' shape which was 100 feet (30 metres) wide. Inside there were three levels of gallery seats so that the punters could get a much better view of Will's marvellous plays.

In fact Shakespeare's Globe looked rather like this:

THE GLOBE THEATRE

THATCHED ROOF - Made of layers of reeds or straw.

GALLERIES - Three levels of seats for those who could afford to pay a bit more.

WALLS - 12 metres tall and covered in lime plaster.

OAK BEAMS - Used to construct the building.

FLOOR - Covered with litter.

GALLERY - Where the musicians sat.

GENTLEMEN'S ROOMS - Or private boxes for very posh people.

YARD - Where the groundlings stood (open to the rain).

STAGE - The stage itself was a rectangular shape that tapered at the front and was big enough for about a dozen actors at the most.

The Secret Diary of William Shakespeare
1599.

Wonderful news! Our new theatre, 'The Globe', has proved to be a big hit! Stealing our old theatre was the best idea that the Burbage brothers ever had. (Apart from making me their chief writer, of course!)

Most new buildings in London these days have tiled roofs, but the Burbage boys have decided to go for a thatched roof instead.

I asked Richard if this was because they thought that a thatched roof would add to the intense emotional atmosphere during performances of my masterpieces. 'No, you dim wit, it's because it's cheaper', he said.

Our new theatre truly is a thing of beauty. No writer could wish for a better setting for his work.

PS Still a bit worried about the roof but, as long as everyone is careful with matches and fire we should be fine!

Richard

104

Eyewitness

One of the earliest records of the theatre in use is by a Swiss visitor to London called Thomas Platter, who in the autumn of 1599 recorded in his diary how he'd just spent the afternoon:

> On September 21st after lunch, about two o'clock, I and my party crossed the water, and there in the house with the thatched roof witnessed an excellent performance of the tragedy of the first Emperor Julius Caesar, very pleasantly performed, with approximately fifteen characters.
>
> Whoever cares to stand below pays only one English penny, but if he wishes to sit he enters by another door, and pays another penny, while if he desires to sit in the most comfortable seats which are cushioned, where he not only sees everything well but can also be seen, then he pays yet another English penny at another door.

Dedicated followers of fashion

Why would people want to pay extra to 'be seen'? Well, in those days posh people didn't go to the theatre just to see the play. (That would be too obvious, wouldn't it?) Rich lords and ladies went to the playhouse so they could show off. They'd pay extra for seats that were in a gallery *behind* the actors on stage. Sitting there made sure that everyone in the crowd could see them grandly wearing their new clothes and jewellery.

Clothes were very important to the Elizabethans as status symbols. They were so important that in 1597 a law was passed which forbade anyone other than nobles from wearing fashionable clothes. The poor weren't allowed to wear ruffs around their necks!

THE WELL-DRESSED GENTLEMEN ABOUT TOWN WORE:

NEATLY KEPT MOUSTACHE

A TRIMMED BEARD

DOUBLET

BREECHES

A STARCHED LINEN RUFF (looks flash but is murder to eat in)

SHORT CLOAK TO JUST BELOW THE WAIST

AND FOR THE LADIES:

FACE PAINTED WHITE

LIPS COLOURED BRIGHT RED

STIFF CORSET - RESTRICTS BREATHING & MOVEMENT

LONG WIDE SKIRT

HAIR WORN UP

In Shakespeare's day men's fashions were just as bright and colourful as women's. Queen Lizzy led the fashion world and whatever she wore was quickly copied by everyone else. Even the colours had colourful names. How would you fancy wearing 'maiden's blush', 'Dead Spaniard', or the very popular 'goose-turd green'?

As fashion was so important it's no surprise that people paid a lot of attention to the costumes that were worn on stage. Clothes were very expensive. For example, a nice gown for a posh lady could cost £7 – that was four months' wages for a schoolteacher.

People liked to see lovely clothes up on stage and as Shakespeare's plays mostly revolved around lords, ladies and kings, the costumes were dead pricey. Some companies found that their wardrobe was worth more money than their theatre. Stealing a costume was the worst thing an actor could ever do – even worse than forgetting his lines!

So if clothes were so expensive, how did Shakespeare and his chums get them? Here's one way...

All the world's a stage

The most important part of any theatre is the stage and the Globe was no exception. Since people were going to be paying their money to stare at it, it had to be impressive. And by golly it was!

PILLARS:
Painted to look like marble, but actually made of wood. (Cheapskates.) They were described as 'painted in such excellent imitation of marble that it is able to deceive even the most cunning'.

STAGE:
The stage itself was carefully placed at an angle where it would always be in shadow. Partly so the sun didn't get in the actors' eyes, and partly because sunlight would have faded the stage's decorations and the performers' expensive costumes.

STAGE ROOF:
This was to keep the actors dry in case it rained. (The audience in the yard just got wet!)

HEAVENS:
This was the name for the underneath of the stage roof and it was one of the most beautiful areas in the theatre. It was painted with images of the sun, the moon, and the circle of the Zodiac, all against a sky-blue background.

'HELL':
The empty space under the stage accessed by a trapdoor. This enabled ghosts or demons to appear as if by magic. The play Hamlet includes the stage direction 'Ghost cries from under the stage'.

109

Shakespeare's special effects

When you think of special effects you probably think of
sci-fi films and monster movies from Hollywood. It might
be surprising but audiences in Shakespeare's time were
treated to quite a few special effects on stage. They were
all designed to astound and astonish the audience and
add to their enjoyment of the play.

Some of Shakespeare's most special effects included:

Bloody sword fights

Actors would use all sorts of tricks to get a bit of blood on
stage. That might sound a bit gory but you have to
remember that people were much more used to such
sights in those days. Many of the audience might have
passed a severed head on a spike on their way to the
theatre for example. Compared to real life the blood on
stage really wasn't so bad.

So how did it work? Well, during a sword fight, for example, one actor might have a sponge soaked in sheep's blood hidden under his arm. When his enemy stabbed him, he would simply squeeze the sponge and blood would suddenly spurt everywhere.

In Shakespeare's *Titus Andronicus* one of the characters is supposed to have had her tongue cut out. The actor playing the part might enter the stage with a mouthful of sheep's blood (ugh!) ready to spit it out on cue.

Sound effects

In a spooky play like Macbeth the sound of menacing thunder would have been added to scenes using a 'thunder run'. No, that wasn't a rude name for someone's trousers. It was a kind of metal trough down which someone rolled a cannonball to create a loud rumbling noise.

Other sound effects were more obvious. For example, to create the sound of firing a cannon, the stagehands would, er ... fire a cannon. The cannon wouldn't be loaded with a real cannonball, of course, but even so it wasn't without its dangers.

One of the plays performed in the early years of the Globe went on to become one of Shakespeare's most popular comedies...

SHAKESPEARE SPOTLIGHT ON...
TWELFTH NIGHT
(OR WHAT YOU WILL)

Written: 1600

Setting: Illyria – an imaginary kingdom far away.

What happens: This play follows two couples: The first, Viola and her twin brother, Sebastian, each think the other has drowned in a shipwreck. The second couple are Duke Orsino and Countess Olivia. Hilarity ensues when Viola disguises herself as a boy (that's *another* boy as girl as boy role), and everybody falls in love with the wrong person. As you'd expect in a comedy, it all ends up happily.

Twelfth Night is particularly loved for its secondary story featuring the character of Malvolio...

Best part: Malvolio. He is Olivia's steward, and he's snooty, vain and has no sense of humour. He is a Puritan (boo!) and a first-class party pooper. Malvolio has one weakness, though; he entertains fantasies that he might woo Olivia himself. He annoys the other characters so much that they decide to set him up. They fake a letter from Olivia saying that she could love him *if* he wore: 1 the colour yellow (which she hates); 2 an odd kind of garter; and 3 a big, big grin.

Olivia sees him, thinks he's gone bonkers, and has him locked up, much to the amusement of everyone else. Malvolio is one of the best comic characters in all of Shakespeare.

Famous quotes:
'Some are born great, some achieve greatness, and some have greatness thrust upon 'em.' Malvolio.
Translation: I can't help being great, me.

'If music be the food of love, play on.' Duke Orsino
Translation: Nothing like a nice tune to put you in the mood.

Food of love

Speaking of music being the food of love … when they were performed, Shakespeare's plays would have had a soundtrack of live music. Music was very important to the Elizabethans and many people played instruments.

In the Globe, the musicians sat on the gallery above the stage. It was a tradition that they should be heard and not seen and so they were usually hidden behind a curtain (so much for being in showbiz).

Will's plays contain over 100 songs which are either sung or listened to by his characters and all the plays (except one) contain stage instructions from Shakespeare himself about the use of music. Sometimes the music was even part of the plot itself. In *King Lear* music is used to calm and soothe the king after he has gone bonkers and bring him back to his senses.

Music would have been used to add atmosphere and excitement to what was happening on stage, just like a film soundtrack does in the cinema today.

Fame and fortune

As the new century began, our Will was at the very top of his profession. He was rich and he was successful. He owned part of an acting company and a theatre. And, probably best of all, his plays were performed to packed audiences who loved them.

In the next decade, Will would go on to produce some of his greatest works. But before he could do that he had to avoid having his head cut off.

SHAKESPEARE AND THE CROWN

It wasn't easy being monarch. Queen Lizzy had a country to run. She had to feed the poor, keep the nobles happy, avoid costly wars, and most of all avoid getting the boot. Although being monarch was a difficult job there were no shortage of people who wanted to get their backsides on the throne. And it wasn't just the dastardly King Philip of Spain, either – some dangers were a *lot* closer to home...

The Earl's rebellion

Robert Devereux, Earl of Essex was a bit of a lad. He'd sailed with Sir Francis Drake in search of Spanish treasure (he didn't find any) and attacked the Spanish at sea with Sir Walter Raleigh. He was great mates with the Queen but they didn't always get on too well.

One day when he returned from a mission in Ireland he burst into the Queen's bedroom unannounced, and saw the Queen without her make-up or wig. Big mistake! The Queen and Essex had a big falling out and he was arrested and sent to prison for a bit. Around that time,

Essex decided that perhaps he might make a better job of ruling the country than Lizzy and started planning a rebellion.

He knew he needed to get the ordinary people on his side and he came up with an idea. He paid Will's company to put on a performance of a play Will had written back in 1595 called *Richard II*. The reason that Essex wanted it performed was that the play shows a king who annoys everyone so much that he eventually has to surrender the crown to someone else.

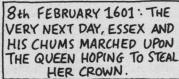

8th FEBRUARY 1601. THE VERY NEXT DAY, ESSEX AND HIS CHUMS MARCHED UPON THE QUEEN HOPING TO STEAL HER CROWN.

GRRR!

FINDING THEIR WAY TO COURT BLOCKED, THE PLOTTERS WENT THROUGH THE CITY LOOKING FOR SUPPORT.

ERR... REBELLION?

NOT TODAY THANKS.

ESSEX REALIZES HE HAS BADLY MISJUDGED THINGS...

GULP

AND BARRICADES HIMSELF IN HIS OWN HOME.

IT SHOULD HAVE BEEN ME! IT SHOULD HAVE BEEN ME!

A FEW WEEKS LATER IT WAS...

OH DEAR.

AND IT WAS CURTAINS FOR SIR GELLY TOO.

EEK

Executions all round

Another member of the plotter's little gang was Henry Wriothesley, the Earl of Southampton and Shakespeare's patron to whom he had dedicated his poems (remember him?). Southampton was sentenced to death, but after his mother did some first-rate grovelling to the Queen and blamed the whole thing on bad boy Essex, the sentence was changed to imprisonment in the Tower.

We know that the Queen wasn't best pleased, either with Essex (obviously), or with Will's company for letting themselves be drawn into the plot. Some people think they were lucky to keep their heads. The Queen must have forgiven them, though, because the day before Essex was due to be executed the company performed a play at court to amuse the Queen. (And you can bet that everyone was trying extra, extra hard.)

The Queen might have (just about) forgiven Shakespeare's company, but she didn't forget. When she was in a bad mood, she was heard to remark later that summer, 'I am Richard II, know ye not that?'

The old Queen had done fantastically well. She'd survived traitors, wars, invasion fleets, and had lived to be 70. Even so she couldn't go on for ever. On 2 February 1603, Shakespeare and the Lord Chamberlain's Men played before the Queen for the last time. Shortly afterwards she fell very ill. (Luckily she didn't blame the play.)

119

THE SHAKESPEAREAN SUN
24 March 1603

THE QUEEN IS DEAD! LONG LIVE THE KING

Queen Lizzy has finally popped her clogs! The shocking news was released from the court today. It was said that she slipped peacefully away after a month-long bout of pneumonia.

The noble lady has done her country proud! Although at the beginning of her reign it was muttered (but not by this newspaper!) that a mere woman would not be up to the job. She has proved all her doubters wrong, spending a royal 45 years upon the throne of England.

Her death leaves a terrible hole in the hearts of her people (and also in our fashion section).

Reports from inside the palace say that the Queen spent her final hours surrounded by anxious councillors waiting for her to name a successor. Finally, the Queen whispered, 'Trouble me no more. Who else but my cousin Scotland?' and then gracefully dropped dead.

So (and as exclusively predicted in your royal reporting Sun last week!) James, King of Scots, is to become James I of England!

The Sun says: Long live the King!

What future for Her Majesty's favourite playwright now?

A fast and well-ordered transition from old monarch to new monarch was vital for the entire country. If things were even slightly delayed, then other people might slip in and try to claim the throne for themselves.

As soon as Lizzy snuffed it, her lady-in-waiting slipped off the sapphire ring from the Queen's finger and dropped it out of the window to a rider waiting on horseback. He covered the 400 miles to Edinburgh in three days and presented the ring to James VI of Scotland, a sign that told him he was now King James I of England as well.

Crown and country

In Shakespeare's day the character of the monarch, and whether they were a good ruler or not, had a very direct effect on the lives of ordinary people. A hasty decision to go to war might mean raising taxes and not enough food, not to mention of course the thousands of soldiers who would be killed on the battlefield. So a king or queen who got the strop could be a real liability to the whole country.

Kings and queens were supposed to have a sacred right of kingship, which was a flash way of saying that they had been chosen by God. The idea that a king was connected to God came from a notion called the Chain of Being. This idea had been inherited from the Middle Ages and it placed every living thing in a strict order of importance or hierarchy. The Chain of Being was supposed to have been created by God, although you might get the mistaken idea it was designed to keep poor people in their place.

The order ran:

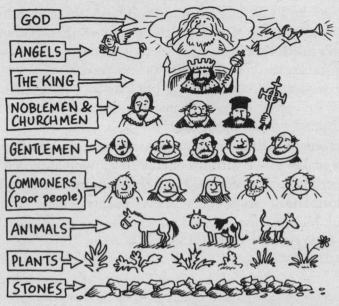

Although the king was supposed to rule by order of God's plan, in practice any king who grew really unpopular with his subjects was likely to be overthrown. As well as being regal, a good king was practical and aware of the needs of his people.

The history plays

The idea that kings and queens have great power but should use it wisely is the subject of many of Will's ten 'history plays'. These plays tell the stories of some of England's rulers and the decisions they made, although Will sometimes altered characters and the timing of events to make a better story. The plays often ask the question *what makes a good king?*

Here's a quick guide to Shakespeare's Kings of England as they are portrayed in his ten history plays:

King John

This play shows King John as an incompetent fool who can't rule for toffee.

I am a clod.

No one likes him – not even the noblemen around him. He makes peace with his enemies by giving away much more than he needs to. Here Shakespeare seems to be asking the question *what if you get an idiot as king?* At the end, John is poisoned, and his son takes over.

Richard II

Like most kings and queens, Richard II believes he has a God-given right to rule, but he upsets everyone else so much that he is murdered and the crown is stolen by the rebel, Henry Bolingbroke.

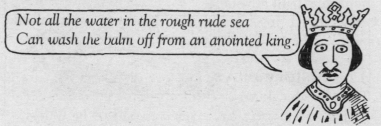

Not all the water in the rough rude sea
Can wash the balm off from an anointed king.

This was the play used by Essex in his failed plot against Queen Lizzy, as we saw on page 117.

Henry IV, Parts 1 and 2

Carrying on from the ending of Richard II, Henry Bolingbroke, now King Henry IV, is ridden with guilt for nicking the crown in the previous play.

Uneasy lies the head that wears a crown.

These two plays are really more about Henry's son, Prince Hal, and the choices he must make as he is growing up. Hal finds he must choose between frittering away his time in taverns with his friend Falstaff, or spending his time and energy on his duties as befits a young prince. In the end he makes the choice to be a leader and, at the end of *Part 2* when his dad kicks the bucket, he becomes King Henry V.

Act fact

One of Shakespeare's most popular characters, Falstaff is such a coward that at one point he lies on a battlefield pretending to be dead so he doesn't have to fight anyone.

The better part of valour is discretion.

One of Falstaff's first fans was said to be Queen Elizabeth. The story goes that she liked the character so much she demanded that Will write a comedy especially featuring him: he did and it was called *The Merry Wives of Windsor*.

The next play is probably the most patriotic of all the historicals…

SHAKESPEARE SPOTLIGHT ON...
HENRY V

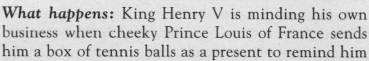

Written: 1599

Setting: England and France.

What happens: King Henry V is minding his own business when cheeky Prince Louis of France sends him a box of tennis balls as a present to remind him of his misspent youth (see previous two plays). Henry V is livid and sets out to invade France. (Yep, just like that.)

Henry V's army arrives on French soil happy enough, but soon his troops are soaking wet, freezing cold and very fed up. Worse still they're about to fight the Battle of Agincourt and are madly outnumbered. Henry V gives a rousing battle speech and inspires his army to a fabulous victory. (In real life, Henry V's army of 13,000 had defeated a French army of 50,000!)

Best part: Henry V. Prince Hal has grown into a wise and effective king. Gone are the days wasted drinking in taverns. He leads his country bravely, but seems harder, more distant, and has little of his human warmth left.

Based on: Holinshed's *Chronicles* which tell the history of England, Scotland and Ireland. Being completely fair and not anti-French at all, Shakespeare portrays the king of France as an idiot.

Famous quotes:
'Cry, "God for Harry! England and Saint George."'
Henry V's famous battle cry.
Translation: Do it for me, lads.

'Once more unto the breach,
Dear friends, once more!' Henry again.
Translation: Do it for me, lads. One more time!

What a performance: Famous Henrys include Lawrence Olivier's flag-waving hero in the 1944 film and Kenneth Branagh's more tortured king in the 1989 movie.

Henry V's replacement as king was a bit of a let-down…

Henry VI, Parts 1, 2 and 3
Although his father Henry V was a great leader, Henry VI is portrayed in this trilogy of plays as a big girl's blouse who lacks backbone. He's not helped by the fact that he's only nine months old when he becomes king. (Talk about early promotion.) He's a kind soul, but is about as useful as a wet flannel when it comes to ruling England.

My crown is in my heart, not on my head.

Henry's weakness eventually leads to the War of the Roses. He dies in the tower at the hands of Richard, Duke of Gloucester, who announces to the audience that he is determined to be king one day. The crown passes to Edward IV (Richard's brother), but we know that the ambitious Richard is lurking in the shadows...

Richard III
As we saw on page 60, Shakespeare's Richard is a poisonous spider who murders his way to the throne. At the end of the play, rascally Richard is killed by Henry Tudor, who becomes Henry VII.

Shakespeare then skipped a king and the last historical play stands apart from the rest.

Henry VIII
Henry VIII was Queen Lizzy's own father, so not surprisingly this isn't exactly a critical look at Henry's character. In fact the character of Henry hardly comes under the spotlight at all, and it's the double-dealing Cardinal Wolsey who is subjected to on-stage dissection.

> *Had I but served my God with half the zeal*
> *I served my king, he would not in mine age*
> *Have left me naked to mine enemies.*

Translation: Darn it. I would have got away with it too, if it wasn't for those pesky nobles.

The play includes many showy set pieces. Will's original stage directions included instructions for lavish costumes, cannon fire and even fireworks.

The head that wears the crown

Apart from the unfortunate nearly-having-your-head-cut-off incident with *Richard II*, Shakespeare and his company had enjoyed a rather chummy and cosy relationship with Queen Lizzy. With her death, that was suddenly all in the past.

Queen Lizzy had been on the throne for 45 years, the whole of Will's life. As the new king began his journey south to London, Shakespeare, like the rest of the country, must have held his breath and wondered what the future had in store...

THE KING'S MAN

Will needn't have worried about the new king too much. As far as his luck was concerned, our Will was still on a roll. It turned out that James I absolutely *loved* the theatre! Just ten days after James got to London he formally adopted Shakespeare's company, the Lord Chamberlain's Men, and changed their name to the *King's* Men. This was great news for Will and his chums.

What wasn't such good news was that shortly after Queen Lizzy's funeral a new outbreak of plague closed all the London theatres. Again. It was so bad that when poor old James was crowned in July no one was allowed to watch him, and the royal procession through the streets scheduled for after the coronation was cancelled.

James I

The new king was married and came with a couple of kids – which was good news as it meant there should be no problems about a successor when James died. He was a nervous little bunny though, and it was said that he often wore padded clothes in case of a surprise assassination attempt! (Must have been hot in the summer.)

James was simply *mad* about the theatre and often saw plays more than once. He liked Will's *The Merchant of Venice* so much that after he'd seen it, he ordered another production at court just two days later! Over the next ten years, Shakespeare and the King's Men performed at court nearly 200 times!

James I also worked out a way of using Shakespeare's talents to further his own cause. Since the defeat of the Spanish Armada in 1588, England and Spain had been in a kind of cold war. Neither side was speaking to the other. Now that Queen Lizzy was gone, it was an ideal opportunity for James I to make peace with England's old enemy.

When the new Spanish ambassador arrived in London the next summer, Shakespeare and the King's Men were hired to entertain him and his travelling party. They were paid a pretty whopping £21.12s for 18 days' work.

The world is not enough

Shakespeare lived in a world that was getting bigger every day. The Elizabethan age had been a time of great exploration. Maps were regularly redrawn to include new lands and new people. In 1604, our Will did a rather brave thing. He wrote a new play that featured a black character as the lead.

It must have been a particularly daring idea at the time. Black Africans were mostly unknown in England and would have been regarded with both suspicion and fascination by your average Londoner. Writing against his audience's expectations, Shakespeare made the sinister villain white and the noble and tragic hero black. The play became one of Shakespeare's classic tragedies...

SHAKESPEARE SPOTLIGHT ON...
OTHELLO

Written: 1604

Setting: Sixteenth-century Venice and Cyprus.

What happens: Othello, an African general in the Venetian army, upsets Iago by passing him over for promotion. Iago gets all hot under the collar and swears revenge. Iago comes up with a cunning plan that's so simple it can't fail. Iago plants the idea in Othello's mind that his beautiful young white wife is having an affair. She's not, but Othello is driven mad with jealousy and kills her. (Oops – maybe writing to an agony aunt first might have been an idea?) When Othello realizes it's all a trick the once noble general tops himself with his own sword.

EEK

It's a straightforward and highly effective plot about two people who really do love each other, but whose relationship falls apart because of suspicion, jealousy, pride and a dirty rotten snake in the grass called Iago.

Best parts: Othello, like all Shakespeare's tragic heroes, is a victim of his own weakness: in Othello's case it is his pride and his over-suspicious mind. Iago's one of Will's all-time great villains. Like Richard III, Will adds to Iago's menacing malevolence by giving him several soliloquies (solo speeches) during which he explains to the anxious audience the nastiness that he intends to do. He seems the perfect soldier to those around him, but Iago's venom poisons Othello's mind against his one true love.

Famous quotes:
'O! beware, my lord, of jealousy:
It is the green-eyed monster which doth mock
The meat it feeds on.' Iago
Translation: Don't get your knickers in a twist (said by Iago while twisting the aforementioned knickers).

What a performance: The first performance of Othello was before King James I on 1 November 1604. It featured the great Richard Burbage in the title role. Although the character is black, Othello was a part usually played by white actors until the twentieth century.

When Margaret Hughes played Desdemona, Othello's wife, in 1660, she was the first woman *ever* to be allowed to act on the stage in England!

Supernatural Shakespeare

Most of the theatre audience would have believed in spells, magic and curses. Most people were superstitious and folklore was likely to be taken at face value. Will's plays reflect the beliefs of the time. They're full of ghosts, witches, spirits and magic. Science was in its infancy, and even people who did study science were often just as interested in witchcraft and the occult as well.

Shakespeare's audiences would have had many beliefs that might seem a little odd today. Which of these weird facts do you think are true – and which are made up?

1 Diamonds are a doc's best friend: Top doctors in Shakespeare's time treated ill patients by grinding expensive jewels into paste and making the patient eat them.

2 Baby baby: People believed that it was dead unlucky to give new clothes to a newborn baby.

3 Horror-scope: Queen Lizzy was such a believer in star signs that she had her own personal astrologer.

4 Bewitched: James I was dead worried his enemies might hire a witch to assassinate him by hexing him with a curse.

5 Midnight snacks: In 1604, James I had the law changed so it became an offence to '*feed any evil or wicked spirit*'.

Answers: They're all completely barmy and they're *all* completely true:

1 It was believed that the more precious (and pricey) the jewel then the better it would work as a remedy. (No wonder most people died young.)

2 People wrapped their newborns in old clothes for at least the first few hours of their lives. (This was a particularly unlucky superstition as old clothes often carried fleas that carried the plague. Doh!)

3 Indeed Queen Lizzy did and his name was Doctor John Dee. He came complete with his own 'magic mirror' and was known as the '*arch conjuror of the whole kingdom*'.

4 This was one of several worries that kept James awake at night.

5 It had been an offence to be in league with the devil for several years, but obviously it was good to close this legal loophole that allowed people just to feed him or his evil friends if they wanted to!

It's witchcraft

Witches were very big business in Will's day. Most of the people accused of being witches were women and the best way of dealing with a witch was to burn her. (Although they were also drowned, hanged and beheaded.)

In 1584, Reginald Scot had written a book entitled *Discovery of Witchcraft* and said that witchcraft had very little to do with the devil and was mostly old ladies fooling people with cheap conjuring tricks. It went directly against what James I believed and annoyed him so much that he wrote his own book on the subject, called *Demonology*, that warned readers of:

> *The fearful abounding at this time in this country of detestable slaves of the devil, the witches.*

With his new royal patron in mind, it wasn't long before our Will came up with a cracker of a tale that not only sucked up to the King's interest in witches but even featured his great-great-great- ... well let's just say it featured his distant ancestor, a chap called Banquo...

Macbeth is one of the most popular plays Shakespeare ever wrote. It's probably no coincidence that it's the equivalent of a seventeenth-century horror film. It's full of murder, ambition, ghosts, witches and blood. Lots and lots of blood.

Round about the cauldron go;
In the poison'd entrails throw.
Toad, that under cold stone
Days and nights hast thirty-one
Swelter'd venom, sleeping got
Boil thou first i' th' charmed pot.
Double, double toil and trouble;
Fire, burn; and cauldron, bubble.

Eye of newt, and toe of frog,
Wool of bat, and tongue of dog,
Adder's fork, and blind-worm's sting,
Lizard's leg, and howlet's wing,
For a charm of powerful trouble,
Like a hell-broth boil and bubble.

Shakespeare Spotlight on...
MACBETH

Written: 1606

Setting: Eleventh-century Scotland.

What happens: On their way home from battle, Macbeth and his friend Banquo meet three witches who foretell that one day Macbeth will become King of Scotland. Sounds nice, eh? The idea takes an obsessive hold of Macbeth's mind and begins to drive him a bit bonkers. His ruthless wife, Lady Macbeth, who is also driven by ambition, nags him until Macbeth murders the sleeping King Duncan who is staying at Macbeth's castle. (Boo! Hiss!)

Macbeth becomes king but things soon begin to go horribly, *horribly* wrong. Macbeth finds that he must commit even more murders to cover up his crime. He tries to keep hold of the crown but it begins to slip through his fingers like a really slippery thing coated in something even more slippery.

Best parts: Macbeth begins the play as a brave and respected soldier, but before long his ambition combines with the malicious meddling of the witches to ensure his downfall. The murder of his close pal Banquo sends Macbeth close to the edge of insanity, and afterwards he sees Banquo's ghost at his supper table. Macbeth is one of Shakespeare's classic tragic heroes: he is a good man when the story starts, but then the witches and Lady Macbeth both play on the one flaw he has – his ambition.

137

Lady Macbeth isn't quite as unfeeling as she'd like to think and the crime haunts her conscience. She spends her final days sleepwalking, obsessively trying to wash her hands of blood that isn't there. The killing of the king haunts Lady Macbeth until she eventually goes completely bonkers and takes her own life.

Based (loosely) on: A real life Macbeth who lived from 1005 to 1057. Shakespeare read about him in Holinshed's *Chronicles*. The historical Macbeth did indeed steal the Scottish throne, but by all accounts reigned happily for 15 years afterwards. (And there's no evidence his wife was involved in the crime.)

Famous quotes:
'Is this a dagger which I see before me…?' Macbeth.
Translation: Oh Gawd, now I'm seeing things. (Macbeth, hallucinating a murder weapon.)

'Life's but a walking shadow; a poor player,
That struts and frets his hour upon the stage,
And then is heard no more; it is a tale
Told by an idiot, full of sound and fury,
Signifying nothing.' Macbeth again.
Translation: I wish I'd never got up this morning.

The curse of Macbeth

Actors are a superstitious lot – perhaps it's something to do with the fact that at any one time, 98% of them are out of work! (That's pretty unlucky.) No surprise then that many believe that *Macbeth* – a play full of witchcraft, evil and murder – is in fact *cursed*! Most actors are so superstitious that they won't even say the 'M word' inside a theatre, preferring to refer to it as 'the Scottish play'.

Any actor who accidentally does say the 'M word' is often thrown out of rehearsals. To get back in they must spin around three times and recite a line from *The Merchant of Venice*: 'Fair thoughts and happy hours attend on you.'

According to legend, the play has been cursed from the very first performance when Hal Berridge, the boy playing Lady Macbeth collapsed backstage with a fever and promptly died.

Accidents happen during the productions of most plays. Is Macbeth any more unlucky than average? *You* decide. Here's just a few disasters supposed to have been caused by the dreaded curse!

1703 - LONDON GETTING HIT BY ONE OF THE WORST STORMS IN HISTORY JUST AFTER A PRODUCTION OF THE PLAY OPENED.

1721 - A FIGHT BREAKING OUT BETWEEN THE CAST AND THE AUDIENCE.

1849 - A RIOT BREAKING OUT IN NEW YORK WHEN 20 PEOPLE GET SHOT BECAUSE CROWDS DISAGREE ABOUT WHO SHOULD PLAY MACBETH.

1882 - ONE MACBETH BEING ACCIDENTALLY STABBED AND SERIOUSLY INJURED DURING A SWORD FIGHT ON STAGE. OUCH!

1934 - A PRODUCTION GETTING THROUGH THREE MACBETHS IN ONE WEEK. ONE ACTOR LOSING HIS VOICE, ANOTHER FALLING ILL WITH A CHILL, AND THE THIRD BEING SACKED AFTER A ROW.

1939 - THE LEAD MAN NEARLY GETTING KILLED, A CAR CRASH, A DEAD DOG, AND THE THEATRE MANAGERESS HAVING A FATAL HEART ATTACK.

1948 - A SLEEPWALKING LADY MACBETH INSISTING ON KEEPING HER EYES SHUT AND FALLING OFF THE CASTLE BATTLEMENTS - OOPS.

SHAKESPEARE'S SUSPECTS

Having just read 140 pages about William Shakespeare and the plays he wrote, it might come as a bit of a shock to be told that some people don't think that he wrote all those dead famous plays at all!

?? MAN OF MYSTERY ??

Some people have suggested that William Shakespeare didn't really write 'his' plays. They think that Will, an actor from out of town, made the perfect front man for someone who didn't want their real identity known. The idea that in fact someone else wrote Shakespeare's plays has been around for hundreds of years and has become known as the 'authorship controversy'.

So, what evidence do these literary detectives have that our Will was involved in this carefully constructed con? Well, they argue, many things about Shakespeare the playwright don't really make sense. 'Like what?' you cry. Well, things like:

1 Brain strain

Will had never been to university or ever travelled abroad, as far as we know, so where did he suddenly get the education to be able to write plays about such varied subject matter? Shakespeare's plays include detailed knowledge of (among many other things): music, plants, classical history, mythology and the legal system. Most of the plays deal with the lives of posh people (often kings – about as posh as you can get). How did lowly out-of-town Will get to find out so many accurate details about what life in a royal court was really like?

2 Unknown at home

It's strange but true, but the people of his hometown, Stratford, don't seem to have known that Shakespeare *was* a writer at all. Considering how successful he was in London, you'd have thought everyone would have known ... unless of course he kept quiet because he hadn't written anything? Oh yes, and one more thing – none of his plays seemed to have been put on in Stratford during his life. Rather odd for a local boy made good?

3 Where there's a will
When he died, Shakespeare didn't leave any letters or diaries that referred to his writing career at all. No one has ever found any early drafts of a play or indeed any play in his handwriting either.

4 Late but not great?
There's no mention of any of his plays or his other writings in Will's will. When he died only a few people paid tribute to him despite the fact that he was very famous. Lesser writers were made much bigger fusses of after their death.

Whodunnit?
Most of this evidence is what detectives would call circumstantial, but it does raise some fair points. So, the big question is this: If Shakespeare didn't write his plays, then who on earth did? It's a mystery that's been called 'history's biggest whodunit'.

Here are some of the Shakespeare suspects whom people have suggested might have been the 'real' Will...

QUEEN ELIZABETH I
As well as being monarch, was Lizzy a right royal writer as well?

1533-1603

Evidence: She was certainly interested in the theatre and actually backed Will's company. She had the brains to do it and the knowledge of royal lifestyles. Another plus point is that if she had wanted to write plays then she could never have done so under her real name – partly because she was Queen and partly because women weren't allowed to. Some people claim that portraits of her and Shakespeare look suspiciously like the same person.

Alibi: Pretty good – after all, she was dead at the time! Well, part of the time. New Shakespeare plays carried on appearing for ten years after the Queen died in 1603.

Verdict: Not guilty.

CHRISTOPHER MARLOWE
One of Shakespeare's
rivals – but was he
Shakespeare too? He
certainly had the
talent.

1564 – 1593

Alibi: Marlowe was
caught up in sixteenth-
century spy games and
was murdered in 1592, before Shakespeare
wrote most of his plays.

Evidence: It has been suggested that Marlowe
faked his own death in order to escape certain
political pressures (he was about to be
arrested at the time!). After that, being
officially dead meant that the only way he
could get his plays performed was to get some
stage stooge to act as a front man. Just about
possible, but would Marlowe have really been
happy for another writer to take the credit?

Verdict: Not guilty.

EDWARD DE VERE, 17TH EARL OF OXFORD

All-round clever posh bloke who would have needed someone a bit lower down on the social scale to act as front man for him. Not a nice person, though. He was said to have once killed a cook and to have done a trouser burp in front of the Queen.

1550-1604

Evidence: There is strong evidence that he wrote plays for Queen Elizabeth in secret so we know he was keen on the theatre (although we don't know if his plays were any good or not). He also loved Italian culture.

Alibi: De Vere would be a much stronger suspect if he hadn't died in 1604 – too early to have written the last nine years' worth of Shakespeare's plays.

Verdict: Not guilty.

NB De Vere was first suggested as a suspect by a schoolteacher from the north of England called Mr Looney. His book company told him that if he wanted to get his idea published in a book then he'd have to change his name!

ROGER MANNERS, 5TH EARL OF RUTLAND.

Well-travelled posh bloke some people think could be in the frame.

1576–1612

Evidence: Records from the Earl's estate show that he paid money to Shakespeare for something, but what? The Earl had travelled to Italy (where many of Will's plays are set). At university the Earl was chums with two Danes called Rosencrantz and Guildenstern – the names of two characters from Hamlet – and he visited the royal court in Denmark just before Hamlet was written.

Alibi: None. The Earl died in 1612 – suspiciously about the same time that Shakespeare stopped writing and suddenly announced his retirement.

Verdict: Case dismissed due to lack of hard evidence.

SIR FRANCIS BACON – THE PRIME SUSPECT

Politician, historian, poet, statesman, philosopher and general smarty-pants.

1561-1623

Evidence: Bacon was certainly a bit of an all-round genius. He had expert legal knowledge, and he knew his plants and gardens too. He also had the right royal connections to have intimate knowledge of the royal court. He might have decided that the safest way to write plays was to use a pen name and have a front man. After all, a really bad review wasn't just bad for box-office takings, it might mean getting your head chopped off!

Some people have read the plays to see if the 'real' author might have left any clues as to his or her identity. One word that does really stand out is the amazing: 'honorificabilitudinitatibus'. (Try saying that with a mouthful of chips.) It appears in a comedy of Will's called Love's Labour's Lost and at 27 letters it's the longest word in the whole of Shakespeare. Some people claim that you can rearrange the letters of that word to read: 'Hic ludi F Baconis nati tuiti orbi' which is Latin for 'These plays, the offspring of F. Bacon, are preserved for the world.'

Alibi: Firstly, we already know that Francis Bacon had a very full and busy life helping run the country. Where would he have got the time to write 38 plays on top of what he was already up to? Secondly, he wasn't a particularly modest man. Shakespeare's plays were very popular in their own time. If you had written some of the most successful plays ever produced, wouldn't you want someone to know about it? If he was worried about getting in trouble for it, he could have put a confession in his will or left a letter to be opened only after his death.

Verdict: Unproven.

Although there are plenty of suspects, frankly there's not a lot of evidence. Until someone comes up with some real evidence, it seems only fair to give the credit for William Shakespeare's plays to, er … William Shakespeare.

MASTER PLAYWRIGHT

James I's reign was a good time for Shakespeare and his company. Will was able to write whatever plays he liked and see them performed by the best actors of his time. Meanwhile, the King's Men enjoyed the enviable position of performing before the court one day, and before a full public theatre the next.

As he grew older, Will may well have made more regular visits home to Stratford. After all, he now owned New Place (that big new house that he'd bought when the money started to roll in). One of the events that would have brought him home to Stratford was a very happy one:

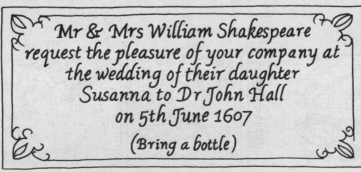

Mr & Mrs William Shakespeare request the pleasure of your company at the wedding of their daughter Susanna to Dr John Hall on 5th June 1607

(Bring a bottle)

As a marriage settlement, well-off Will gave Susanna a very big gift of over 100 acres of land in Stratford. Not a bad present from someone who started out as a glove-maker's son!

Maybe Will was inspired by his daughter's love match, because around that time Will wrote *Antony and Cleopatra*. It was written around the same period as *Macbeth* and *Othello*, and follows their examples by showing what happens to a great and noble man (Antony) when his inner feelings (love for Cleo) clash with his public role (love for Rome).

Maybe this was how our Will felt about something that was happening in *his* life: the fact that he had to stay in London to be a playwright, but that his heart really belonged in Stratford with his wife and children. Well, *perhaps*, but we'll never really know.

The ending has a bit in common with the others too.

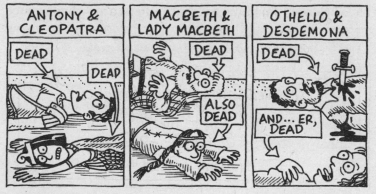

Blackfriars at last

Remember that theatre in Blackfriars (page 95) that Will and the company nearly moved into before they nicked the wood and built the Globe? Well in 1609 the company finally got its way and took it over. So what was wrong with the lovely Globe you might ask? Well, the Globe was great for summer but you must bear in mind one little detail. It didn't have a roof.

Winters in those days were cold enough to freeze over the Thames, so standing around in the wet and the cold wasn't too popular. With an indoor theatre though, the company could perform at the Globe in the summer and then move to Blackfriars for the winter, so they could perform *all* year.

A ROOF

Blackfriars Theatre only held 700 punters as compared to the Globe's 3,000, *but* as it was indoors the company could charge six times more for each ticket (sixpence instead of the penny it cost to be a groundling).

The company created a syndicate to own the new theatre just as they had for the Globe. The lucky group consisted of seven people including our Will. Each member of the syndicate had to pay just over £5 every year to contribute to the cost of renting the theatre which was £40. It was a very good deal, though. Thanks to the increased seat prices, the new theatre made double the profit that the Globe did. It was so popular that it caused one of London's first ever traffic jams.

The same year that Will and company finally got their mitts on Blackfrairs Theatre all the theatres in London were ordered to close again. Guess why? (Clue: It's six letters, begins with 'p' and kills people.)

More comedies

Perhaps because Shakespeare was getting older (he was nearly 50), Will's next few works were all about *reunions*.

CYMBELINE - AN OLD MAN'S SONS REAPPEAR HAVING BEEN LOST FOR MOST OF HIS LIFE. (BLESS.)

FATHER! SONS!

PERICLES - YOUNG MARINA ESCAPES FROM PIRATES AND FINDS HER FATHER AGAIN. (HOORAY!)

ARR! FATHER! DAUGHTER!

THE WINTER'S TALE - A KING MEETS HIS LOST DAUGHTER AND IS ALSO REUNITED WITH HIS QUEEN TOO WHO HAD, UM...BEEN TURNED INTO A STATUE. (WHAT ARE THE CHANCES OF THAT HAPPENING?)

FATHER! DAUGHTER! HUSBAND!

Another play about people finding each other again was...

SHAKESPEARE SPOTLIGHT ON ..
THE TEMPEST

Written: 1611

Setting: A magical island in a faraway ocean.

What happens: Prospero used to be Duke of Milan, but got chucked out and marooned on a distant island by his naughty brother. Since getting stuck on the island old Prospero has spent the years studying and is now a powerful magician. When his naughty brother sails near the island, Prospero plays weatherman and sends a big storm to shipwreck him. Now that naughty bro is also trapped on the same island as Prospero, will the magician take his revenge on his dirty Dukedom-nicking brother or will he forgive him?

Best parts: Prospero grows in wisdom and finally leaves the island a more compassionate man. Ariel: a spirit of the air who Prospero discovered trapped inside a tree. Prospero freed Ariel to be his slave although now Ariel longs to earn her freedom from him. Caliban: another of Prospero's slaves, who's said to be the child of a witch and a sea monster.

Based on: *The Tempest* was probably inspired by real life. The year before Will had read about a ship called the *Sir George Somers* being wrecked near the Bermudas. It was the age of exploration and brave voyagers being shipwrecked in mysterious places was quite the fashion.

Famous quotes:
'...O brave new world
That hath such people in't!' Miranda (Prospero's daughter), about seeing her first boy.
Translation: Blimey. I'll have some of that.

What a performance: Several films including one rather marvellous science-fiction flick in 1956 called *Forbidden Planet* where the enchanted island is replaced by the mysterious planet, Altair-4. Prospero is transformed into the dotty scientist, Dr Mobius, and his supernatural slave, Ariel, becomes a computerized assistant, Robby the Robot.

ALL HAIL, GREAT MASTER; GRAVE SIR, HAIL! I COME TO ANSWER THY BEST PLEASURE...

??MAN OF MYSTERY??

It's been suggested that Prospero was modelled on Shakespeare himself. Was the master storyteller thinking about giving up writing and retiring back to Stratford?

SHAKESPEARE

MASTER STORYTELLER

GIVES UP PLAY-WRITING

LEAVES ADOPTED HOME OF LONDON

RETURNS HOME AGAIN

PROSPERO

MASTER MAGICIAN

GIVES UP MAGIC

LEAVES ADOPTED HOME OF ISLAND

RETURNS HOME AGAIN

Towards the end of the play, Prospero asks the audience to applaud and so release him from the spell he's under ... was that Shakespeare's way of asking to be released from the spell that the theatre had cast upon him?

Our revels now are ended. These our actors,
As I foretold you, were all spirits, and
Are melted into air, into thin air...
...We are such stuff
As dreams are made on; and our little life
Is rounded with a sleep.

THE FINAL CURTAIN

We don't know exactly when Will decided to retire and move back home to Stratford. The nearest we can get for certain is sometime between 1611 and 1613. We don't know the exact reason either.

?? MAN OF MYSTERY ??

Did Will finally decide that he'd had enough of the smells and dangers of London life? Did he want to spend more time with his family? Or had he simply written as much as he cared to and decided he needed a good rest? After all, he was now nearly 50 which was a good age for those days.

Will's replacement

The company got in another writer to replace Will. He was the up-and-coming John Fletcher. Will stayed around long enough to show John the ropes and the two of them wrote three plays together; *Henry VIII*, *Cardenio* (now lost) and *Two Noble Kinsmen*. *Two Noble Kinsmen* is a bit of a patchwork and it's pretty easy to spot the scenes that our Will wrote because he always used much more colourful and complicated language than the younger Fletcher. John Fletcher went on to co-write plays with Francis Beaumont and for a while (well, the next 100 years) their plays were just as popular (at least) as our Will's! Fletcher died in 1625.

Flaming heck

In the summer of 1613, something terrible happened to the Globe that Will had now left behind...

THE SHAKESPEAREAN SUN
29 June 1613
WHAT A PERFORMANCE!

Disaster stuck at the Globe today when the entire building was burnt to the ground! The tragedy happened during a performance of William Shakespeare's Henry VIII.

The inferno was caused by a cannon being fired to announce the arrival of King Henry on stage. The cannon misfired, and set light to the theatre's thatched roof! At first the actors tried to carry on with the performance, but the fire spread quickly along the thatch and soon all 3,000 members of the audience had to flee.

Amazingly, though, everyone got out alive. 'One man had his trousers set alight,' reported posh bloke Sir Henry Wotton. 'With some quick thinking, he put out the fire with a bottle of beer!'

The entire building burnt to the ground in less than an hour.

The Puritans and other people who didn't like the theatre said that it was an act of God and 'Ha ha ha'. But then they would, wouldn't they?

There's also a story that actor John Hemings was seen rushing around the burning building grabbing the play scripts. Maybe it was his quick thinking that saved all Will's works from going up in flames with the rest of the theatre!

A new Globe

Under the terms of the lease, the shareholders (including Shakespeare) had a duty to 'maintain and repair' the building. As it had burnt down, that meant they had a legal obligation to rebuild it. That was going to be quite a pricey business. Each shareholder had to pay the sum of £50 to start the work – although the final cost came to much more. While the company played its winter season in the Blackfriars Theatre, a brand new Globe was rebuilt on the ashes of the old. This time it had a roof of fire-proof tiles and *not* thatch. By the next summer it was open for business as usual. This version of the Globe survived for the next 30 years until it was finally closed down by order of the top Puritan party pooper, Oliver

Cromwell, in 1642. The building itself was finally torn down in 1644, having given audiences many, many afternoons of entertainment. (It would be well over 400 years before yet another Globe would be built, but we'll get to that a bit later.)

Where there's a will

In January 1616, our Will called in his lawyer and asked him to draw up his, er … will. Shakespeare signed it in March. Here's how Will's will split things up:

> To my dear wife, I leave the second best bed.
>
> To Susanna, my eldest daughter, I leave all my other property including New Place.
>
> To Judith, my younger daughter, I leave £300 and my best silver-gilt bowl. (Remember to polish it.)
>
> To my dear friends from the King's Men, Richard Burbage, Henry Condell, and John Heminges, I leave enough money to buy a gold mourning ring in my memory.
>
> To William Walker, my Godson, I leave 20 shillings in gold.

To Joan, my sister, I leave £20, all my clothes, and the use of the house in Henley Street for the rest of her life.

To her three sons (my dear nephews) I leave £5 each.

And to the poor of Stratford, I leave a donation of £10.

The most famous line in the will is what he left to his wife: the 'second best bed'. Some people have suggested that if that's all she got then Will couldn't have loved her very much. In fact, that's probably not how it worked. As his wife, the law entitled Anne to a full third of his entire estate for the rest of her life – so he didn't need to mention that in the will. She probably got the 'second best bed' because that was her personal favourite.

Many experts think that the signatures reveal that Will wasn't very well. The person signing the document (and it needed signing on every page) started well, but the signatures soon lapsed into a weak and untidy scrawl. William Shakespeare was dying.

A little while after signing the new will, Shakespeare fell ill with a fever. On 23 April 1616 (probably his 52nd birthday) the greatest writer of all time died. He was buried in Holy Trinity Church in his hometown of Stratford-upon-Avon. Shakespeare wrote his epitaph for his tombstone. (Well, he would, wouldn't he?)

> GOOD FRIEND, FOR JESUS' SAKE FORBEAR
> TO DIG THE DUST ENCLOSED HERE;
> BLEST BE THE MAN THAT SPARES THESE STONES
> AND CURST BE HE THAT MOVES MY BONES.

The threat of the curse on anyone who moved Will's bones certainly worked. No one ever did.

?? MAN OF MYSTERY ??

Some people have wondered if that meant that there was a secret buried with Shakespeare? Maybe a half-finished play or two? Or maybe the secret identity of that mystery lady from the sonnets? We'll never know. It's quite likely though that our Will was more worried about being dug up and moved to make way for another burial than he was about hiding secrets.

In 1623, his family decided to mark Will's last resting place by commissioning a special painted statue of him. The stone bust showed Will with a quill in hand and was sculpted by Gerard Jassen, a stonemason from London. Since the family approved the statue, it must have been a good likeness, maybe the best we have.

After 52 years, and 37 plays, Will was dead. Or was he? In fact Shakespeare's death was just the beginning. Our Will was going to survive well into the twenty-first century. He'd become the king of Hollywood. In fact, he would eventually conquer the entire globe … and here's how he did it…

Friends indeed

Two of Will's pals were determined to make sure that he wasn't forgotten. John Hemings and Henry Condell (both actors from the King's Men) got together the texts from 36 of Will's plays and had them published in one leather-bound folio. (A 'folio' was a large book.) Some of Will's plays had been in print before this, but these cheap editions were not official and were often made from notes secretly taken during performances or from scripts nicked from the theatre.

'The First Folio' was printed in November 1623, and sold for the sum of £1. The first page announced:

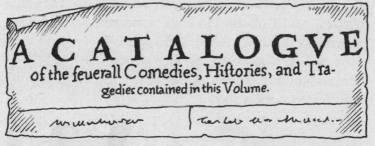

The Folio included a list of actors who had performed the plays at the Globe, and a nice engraved picture of our Will. Around 200 copies of the First Folio are still knocking around. And as you'd expect, there're worth a pretty penny – how does *four million quid* a copy sound?

Henry and John said that their aim was 'only to keep the memory of so worthy a friend, and fellow alive, as was our Shakespeare'. Will's two friends certainly managed that.

Our final spotlight puts Shakespeare's greatest play (and probably the most important and influential play *ever* written) centre stage…

SHAKESPEARE SPOTLIGHT ON…
HAMLET

Written: 1601

Setting: The royal court of Denmark.

What happens: The ghost of Hamlet's father appears and tells Hamlet that he was murdered by his brother, Claudius (Hamlet's uncle). SHOCK! Claudius has nicked the throne *and* married Hamlet's mother. (Now that *was* a busy day.) Hamlet is understandably a bit put out and vows revenge.

After that, well, things get a bit messy…

- Hamlet accidentally stabs his girlfriend Ophelia's father through a curtain. (Oops.)

EEK!

- Ophelia goes bonkers and drowns herself. (Gulp.)

- Claudius gives Laertes (Ophelia's brother) a poisoned sword to use on Hamlet in a duel but their swords get mixed up and Laertes dies instead. (Double oops.)

- At the same time Claudius also gives Laertes a cup of poison for Hamlet to drink in case the sword doesn't work. But don't worry; Laertes doesn't drink the poison by accident. Oh no. Hamlet's mum, the Queen, drinks the poison by accident instead. (Double gulp.)

- A wounded Hamlet finally manages to get his revenge (that's what this was all about, remember?) and kills the evil, throne-stealing Claudius.

- Hamlet is then proclaimed king, makes a full recovery and lives happily ever after. Well, no actually he doesn't. He dies from his wounds as well. (This is a tragedy, remember?)

Best part: Hamlet is probably the best part in the whole of Shakespeare! (Certainly the longest – Hamlet has over 1,500 lines to learn for the four-hour play!) Hamlet is the most complex of all Shakespeare's characters and playing him is usually considered the very peak of an actor's career. He delivers several key soliloquies in which he ponders the meaning of life. And that's his trouble, really. He thinks too much and acts too little. Throughout the play he puts off and delays taking his revenge. *Hamlet* was once billed as 'the story of a man who cannot make up his mind'.

Based on: An ancient story by Saxo Grammaticus (that's his *name* by the way, not how he wrote) telling the history of Denmark.

Famous quotes: No other play has given the English language so many quotes and phrases. It's packed with stuff like: 'Though this be madness, yet there be method in it,' and 'I must be cruel only to be kind.' And it contains what is probably the most famous quote in all of Shakespeare:

To be, or not to be;
that is the question:
Whether 'tis nobler in the mind
to suffer
The slings and arrows of
outrageous fortune,
Or to take arms against a sea of
troubles,
And, by opposing, end them?

Translation: I might do better to top meself…

What a performance: Hamlet has all the ingredients of a classic revenge tragedy: a ghost, people going insane, lovers breaking up, a sword fight, poison and murder, lots of murder. No wonder it was an immediate hit, especially with our old friend Richard Burbage playing the title role, and (it was said) Will himself playing the spooky spectre of Hamlet's father.

SHAKESPEARE THROUGH THE CENTURIES

Our Will might have been dead but thanks to his works (and, as we've seen, his friends) he was going to be remembered for some time to come. Here's a quick guide to how Will has survived the last 400 years and what people have done to (sorry – should that be '*with*') his works since then.

Seventeenth century (1600s)

As we've seen, the killjoy Puritans (boo!) finally succeeded in taking over the country and managed to close ALL London's theatres permanently in 1642. (And no, if you had a ticket you didn't get a refund!)

But never fear, it didn't last long. The theatres were reopened when the monarchy returned in the Restoration…

Even though there were loads of new plays, our Will wasn't forgotten and was still very, very popular. But it wasn't all good news. Some Restoration writers thought that our Will's works could do with a bit of improving and heavily rewrote them. (Cheeky beggars.) Will wouldn't have been too happy about that.

The cheeky chappies who did the rewriting were William Davenant and Nahum Tate. They liked to give Shakespeare's tragedies a happy ending (seeing as how they were all tragic and that) so everyone tended to be alive and smiling at the end. (In Tate's version of *Macbeth*, Macbeth doesn't kill King Duncan but gives him a fluffy bunny instead. Well, not quite, but you get the point.)

Eighteenth century (1700s)

Shakespeare performances in the eighteenth century meant one man – David Garrick. He was absolutely bonkers about our Will and even had a temple to him in his garden. Garrick was an actor-manager, which meant that he not only starred on the stage but that he ran the theatre as well.

Garrick was on a mission to get Shakespeare known to an even wider audience. In his lifetime (1717–1779) he produced nearly all of Will's plays and starred in most of them as well. It was said that he introduced a more realistic style of acting to the stage, and he took just as many liberties rewriting Will as other people had.

Towards the end of his life (1769) Garrick organized what he called a 'Shakespeare Jubilee' in Stratford-upon-Avon. It was the beginning of what is now a multi-million-pound Shakespeare industry based in the town. Garrick's three-day Jubilee had its good points and its not-quite-so-good points:

GOOD POINTS

Masquerade ball
Songs celebrating our Will
Cannon salutes
Fireworks

NOT-QUITE-SO-GOOD POINTS

Torrential rainstorm
River Avon bursts its banks

None of Will's plays were actually performed at the festival, but it did get lots of publicity and helped establish Shakespeare's reputation right across Europe.

Nineteenth century (1800s)

After a couple of hundred years, people stopped messing about with the scripts and returned to the proper versions of Will's plays. (About time!)

Shakespeare's birthplace in Henley Street in Stratford was put up for sale in 1847 and was nearly shipped over to America! There was a plan to move the entire house brick by brick. (Maybe they'd read the story about Will nicking that theatre?) In the end, though, the house stayed where it was. During the sale it was advertised as 'the most honoured monument of the greatest genius that ever lived' – but that's estate agents for you.

The trend on the stage in the nineteenth century was to try to be as historically accurate as possible. Stage sets became very realistic and sometimes included live animals and features like real waterfalls. (Things could get a bit damp if you were in the front row.) No expense was spared and battle scenes sometimes used hundreds of extras as soldiers.

Twentieth century (1900s)

Productions in the twentieth century tended to return to simpler sets. As Shakespeare grew more popular around the world, so producers and directors often tried to bring a new angle to bear on the master's work. Here's a few of the more unusual takes on Will's works:

Shakespeare goes to Hollywood

Will's timeless stories have made him a huge hit in Tinseltown. Hollywood producers have made more versions of Will's classics than any other single writer.

Apart from the straight adaptations of his plays, they have also been used as the jumping-off point for musicals like *West Side Story*, science-fiction tales like *Forbidden Planet*, and modern retellings like *Ten Things I Hate About*

You which moved the action of *The Taming of the Shrew* to an American high school. Will is so famous that he's even appeared as a fictional character himself. The 1998 movie *Shakespeare in Love* is a light-hearted comedy that tells the story of a young Shakespeare falling in love against the backdrop of the writing and performance of *Romeo and Juliet*. The film went on to win seven Oscars. Four hundred years after he died, Shakespeare had become the biggest writer in Hollywood!

Another new Globe

Late in the twentieth century an amazing thing happened to Shakespeare's Globe Theatre. After a gap of nearly 400 years, another Globe was built on the banks of the River Thames in London. Here's how:

1949: American actor and Shakespeare lover, Sam Wanamaker, visits London. He searches the southern bank of the Thames for a monument to his favourite writer, but finds only a little plaque on the side of a brewery. Sam decides that this isn't a very fitting monument for the greatest writer in the world and makes a big decision. He vows to build a replica of the Globe on Bankside, as close as possible to where the original stood.
1969: Sam sets about persuading people it's a good idea, and raising money.
1970–86: Sam finds a site on the South Bank only to have it taken away again. He fights his corner and wins.
1987: Building work begins. Traditional craftsmen are used as much as possible, slowly creating the theatre from bricks, oak, thatch and putty – as it would have been in Shakespeare's day. The walls are covered with

Elizabethan plaster made of sand, lime and animal hair. The Globe becomes the first building in London to have a thatched roof since the Great Fire of 1666. (Although with a modern sprinkler system!)

1989: Archaeologists locate part of the original Globe and learn a lot more about its size and shape. Building plans are changed to take account of the new discoveries so that the new version of the Globe can be as close to the original as possible.

1993: Sam dies, but his project is well on the way to becoming a reality.

1997: The Globe officially opens as the actress Zoë Wanamaker (Sam's daughter) steps on stage to read the Prologue to our Will's *Henry V*.

The new Globe cost over 20 million pounds to build. Each year, there's a summer season of Will's plays at the Globe and also the world's biggest permanent exhibition all about Shakespeare. Throughout the whole year the Globe runs workshops and classes for schools, and groups can tour backstage and learn all about Will and his works in the theatre that they were written to be performed in.

Shakespeare in space

It might sound unlikely, but our Will's influence stretches right up into space. Yep, Shakespeare has boldly gone where no playwright has gone before … all the way to Uranus, one of the outer gas giants of the solar system.

Uranus has 20 moons and 15 of them are named after characters from our Will's works. Orbiting around Uranus you'll find: *The Tempest*'s Ariel, Caliban and Miranda, as well as Oberon, Titania and Puck from *A Midsummer Night's Dream*. Joining them spinning through space are *Hamlet*'s Ophelia, *Othello*'s Desdemona, and there's even a moon named for the romantic Juliet. (But none for Romeo!)

A final bow

In the introduction to the first printing of Shakespeare's works, Ben Jonson wrote: 'He was not of an age, but for all time.' He couldn't have known how true those words would prove to be.

Shakespeare's Complete Works:

1590-91 Henry VI, Part 1, 2 and 3

1592   Richard III, Titus Andronicus,
       Venus and Adonis (poem)

1593   The Comedy of Errors,
       The Taming of the Shrew,
       The Rape of Lucretia (poem),
       Sonnets – work begins

1594   The Two Gentlemen of Verona,
       Love's Labour's Lost

1595   Romeo and Juliet, Richard II

1596   A Midsummer Night's Dream, King John

1597   The Merchant of Venice, Henry IV, Part 1

1598   Henry IV, Part 2,
       The Merry Wives of Windsor

1599   Henry V, Much Ado About Nothing,
       Julius Caesar

1600   As You Like It, Twelfth Night

1601   Hamlet

1602   Troilus and Cressida, Sonnets completed

1603   All's Well That Ends Well,
       Measure for Measure

1604   Othello

1605   Timon of Athens

1606   King Lear, Macbeth

1607   Anthony and Cleopatra, Coriolanus

1608   Pericles

1609   Cymbeline

1610   The Winter's Tale

1611   The Tempest

1612   Henry VIII (with John Fletcher),
       Two Noble Kinsmen (with John Fletcher)